JOURNAL FOR THE STUDY OF THE OLD TESTAMENT SUPPLEMENT SERIES

62

Editors
David J A Clines
Philip R Davies

JSOT Press
Sheffield

THE
OLD TESTAMENT
AND
FOLKLORE STUDY

Patricia G. Kirkpatrick

Journal for the Study of the Old Testament
Supplement Series 62

IN MEMORY OF

JWK

Copyright © 1988 Sheffield Academic Press

Published by JSOT Press
JSOT Press is an imprint of
Sheffield Academic Press Ltd
The University of Sheffield
343 Fulwood Road
Sheffield S10 3BP
England

Typeset by Sheffield Academic Press
and
printed in Great Britain
by Billing & Sons Ltd
Worcester

British Library Cataloguing in Publication Data

Kirkpatrick, Patricia G.
  The Old Testament and folklore study.—
  (Journal for the study of the Old
  Testament supplement series; ISSN 0309-
  0787; 62).
  1. Bible. O.T.—Hermeneutics
  I. Title   II. Series
  221.6′7   BS1180.2

ISBN 1-85075-114-5
ISBN 1-85075-113-7-Pbk

CONTENTS

Preface	7
Abbreviations	9
Introduction	11

Chapter 1
THE INFLUENCE OF FOLKLORE STUDIES ON
CRITICAL APPROACHES TO THE OLD TESTAMENT 13

1. Folklore Studies and the Old Testament	13
2. What is Folklore?	15
3. Folklore Research and its Influence on Old Testament Studies	17
4. The Documentary Hypothesis	18
5. Hermann Gunkel and the Form-Critical Search for an Oral Text	23
6. Tradition-Historical Approaches and the Assumption of Faithful Transmission	34
a. Albrecht Alt	34
b. G. von Rad and M. Noth	36
c. Folkloré and the *Urtext*	44
d. Scandinavian Scholarship	45
7. Has Progress been Made in the Understanding of Oral Composition and Transmission?	49

Chapter 2
FOLK NARRATIVE:
ITS COMPOSITION AND TRANSMISSION 51

1. Oral Narrative Composition	51
2. Oral Narrative Transmission	65
3. Implications for the Study of the Patriarchal Narratives of the Old Testament	72

Chapter 3
FOLKLORE STUDIES AND THE GENRE
OF THE PATRIARCHAL NARRATIVES   73
  1. 'Verbal Art' and the Classification of
     Written Prose Narrative   73
     a. Genre Classification   74
     b. *Sage*/Saga/Legend/*Legende*   75
     c. Prose Narrative Categories   76
  2. Folk Narrative and the Biblical Text   90
  3. Genre Classification and History   97
     a. Oral History and the Patriarchal Narratives   98
     b. Oral Traditions and Historical Reliability   101
     c. Conclusions   110
  4. General Conclusions   112

Chapter 4
CONCLUSIONS   115

Notes   119
Bibliography   139
Index of Authors   151

PREFACE

The present work was originally written as part of a doctoral thesis submitted to the University of Oxford in 1984. I am greatly indebted to my former supervisor the Rev. Dr E.W. Nicholson, Oriel Professor of the Interpretation of Holy Scripture, for his continued interest in and support of this research topic. For his comments and criticisms I am sincerely grateful. Of course there are many others without whose support this book would not have reached its present form. To my parents and sisters, none of whom ever doubted that one day the work would reach completion, I owe my thanks for their encouragement. For the many friends who offered every kind of support imaginable I thank my God. I am, however, particularly grateful to the Rev. Dr M.E. Isaacs of Heythrop College, London University, who has seen this work at every one of its stages, and has given so freely of her time and scholarly experience. I do not exaggerate when I say that had it not been for her endless patience and generous support this particular tale would never have been written.

Patricia G. Kirkpatrick

Faculty of Religious Studies
McGill University, Montreal
July, 1987

ABBREVIATIONS

Bib	*Biblica*
BTB	*Biblical Theology Bulletin*
BKAT	Biblischer Kommentar, Altes Testament
BWA(N)T	Beiträge zur Wissenschaft vom Alten (und Neuen) Testament
BZ	*Biblische Zeitschrift*
BZAW	Beihefte zur Zeitschrift für die alttestamentliche Wissenschaft
CJT	*Canadian Journal of Theology*
CBQ	*Catholic Biblical Quarterly*
Dis.Ab.	*Dissertation Abstracts*
ET	English translation
ExpT	*Expository Times*
FFC	Folklore Fellows Communications
FOTL	Forms of Old Testament Literature
FRLANT	Forschungen zur Religion und Literatur des Alten und Neuen Testaments
HKAT	Handkommentar zum Alten Testament
HTR	*Harvard Theological Review*
HUCA	*Hebrew Union College Annual*
Int.	*Interpretation*
JAF	*Journal of American Folklore*
JAOS	*Journal of the American Oriental Society*
JBL	*Journal of Biblical Literature*
JFI	*Journal of the Folklore Institute*
JJS	*Journal of Jewish Studies*
JQR	*Jewish Quarterly Review*
JSOT	*Journal for the Study of the Old Testament*
JSS	*Journal of Semitic Studies*
JTS	*Journal of Theological Studies*
MT	Masoretic text
NLH	*New Literary History*
OED	*Oxford English Dictionary*
OTL	Old Testament Library

PMLA	Proceedings of the Modern Language Association
RB	Revue Biblique
RGG	Die Religion in Geschichte und Gegenwart
SBT	Studies in Biblical Theology
SFQ	Southern Folklore Quarterly
SVT	Supplements to Vetus Testamentum
ThZ	Theologische Zeitschrift
VT	Vetus Testamentum
VTS	Vetus Testamentum, Supplement series
ZAW	Zeitschrift für die alttestamentliche Wissenschaft
ZThK	Zeitschrift für Theologie und Kirche

Text and Translations
The Hebrew text cited throughout this work is that of *Biblia Hebraica Stuttgartensia*, ed. K. Elliger and W. Rudolph (Stuttgart, 1968-). The English translation of the Old Testament has been taken from the *Revised Standard Version*.

INTRODUCTION

It has long been a premiss of Old Testament scholarship that behind much of the biblical material lies an oral literature. Many of the major attempts to reconstruct 'Israel's' pre-history have relied upon the assumption that behind the patriarchal narratives lies material which was originally oral in composition and subsequently transmitted by word of mouth over an extended period of time. Therefore, it is hardly surprising that Old Testament scholars have turned to the findings of folklore studies in order to understand the nature of oral literature, its composition and transmission.

It is almost a century since the pioneers of such an interdisciplinary approach began their work. Since that time neither biblical nor folklore scholarship has stood still. Many of the conclusions previously arrived at by folklorists have now been either abandoned or considerably modified. It is, therefore, imperative that biblical scholars should not only be aware of contemporary folklore research, but also, in the light of its findings, revise their own theories concerning the possibility of recovering a presumed original oral form of the biblical text.

This work will explore, not only the use of folklore studies by biblical scholars of the past, but also the implications of contemporary folklore research for present day theories of the composition and transmission of the patriarchal narratives.

Chapter 1

THE INFLUENCE OF FOLKLORE STUDIES ON CRITICAL APPROACHES TO THE OLD TESTAMENT

1. *Folklore Studies and the Old Testament*

The extent to which Old Testament scholars are indebted to many of the presuppositions and conclusions of Folklore Studies is well known. In the past century it has frequently been the case that the questions and debates within one discipline have been paralleled in the other. The reason for this is quite straightforward, namely, both disciplines were concerned with the sociological and historical environment in which various oral and written traditions had been composed and transmitted. It is not surprising to find, therefore, that in their attempts to write the history of ancient Israel, Old Testament scholars frequently turned to the methods of contemporary folklorists to aid them in their reconstructions.

It was J.G. Frazer's *Folk-lore in the Old Testament*, published in 1918,[1] which was the first study to acknowledge the relationship between these two disciplines. It was also the first attempt to assess the extent to which the Old Testament contained elements of folklore. Frazer's methods were largely comparative, and whereas his work has received criticism for its evolutionary view of human societies it is nonetheless a veritable mine of folklore material.[2]

The scope of the work was determined in large part by the all-inclusive definition of folklore which Frazer accepted:

> long after the majority of men in a community have ceased to think and act like savages, not a few traces of the old ruder modes of life and thought survive in the habits and institutions of the people. Such survivals are included under the head of folklore which in the broadest sense of the word may be said to embrace the whole body of a people's traditional beliefs and customs so far as these appear

to be due to the collective action of the multitude and cannot be traced to the individual influence of great men.[3]

By adopting a comparative approach, Frazer isolated a number of beliefs and customs in the Old Testament which he argued were vestiges of more ancient practices. Frazer's essential presupposition was that each culture underwent the same process of evolution, albeit at different rates. Cultures from anywhere in the world would thus react in the same way and would produce similar literature and other art forms, which could be compared.[4] In this way Frazer was able to accumulate comparative material with which to prove the antiquity of various customs described in the Old Testament, and went on to argue that certain of these customs had been observed during a patriarchal age. Thus the authors of the patriarchal narratives were either describing what they themselves had witnessed or were writing down customs which had been preserved by oral tradition.[5] Frazer's acceptance of the Jacob narratives as biographical is indicative of his assumption that oral tradition can be and is a trustworthy carrier of ancient beliefs and customs.[6] It goes without saying that such views would affect questions of historicity.[7] What is intriguing to note is that Frazer never concerned himself with the mechanisms of oral transmission. He simply accepted the presupposition that societies create their own means of oral transmission and that they form an integral part of any definition of folklore. Nevertheless, Frazer did not hold to a rigidly defined theory concerning the reliability of oral transmission. In fact the issue of the dependability of oral transmission is never discussed by him. A careful reading of his work indicates that he adopted theories of both degeneration and preservation in oral transmission, depending upon the circumstances. In some instances he accepted that the biblical narrative had preserved a reliable account of the events portrayed, whilst in other instances only the vestiges of ancient tradition had been recorded. So, for example, when Jacob puts on goatskins in order to deceive his father (Genesis 27), according to Frazer this was a reminiscence of an ancient legal ceremony. Here the Old Testament narrative contained a 'degenerate form' of an 'ancient rite', which, although recounted, had been misunderstood by the biblical author.[8] With regard to Jacob's marriage however, Frazer's conclusions were quite different. In this instance, he made recourse to ancient and contemporary analogies, and argued that oral tradition had faithfully preserved the details of an ancient tradition.[9]

1. Folklore Studies and Old Testament Criticism 15

Nevertheless, in both examples Frazer maintained that, albeit to greater or lesser extent, aspects of a more ancient tradition had survived through oral tradition. It would not be fair, however, to depict Frazer's inconsistent and arbitrary use of differing and sometimes opposing theories of oral transmission as a reflection of the position of most folklorists of his day. His readiness to adopt either degeneration or preservation theories of oral transmission obscures the real debate in folklore studies, where those who upheld the theory of degeneration and those who emphasized the reliability of oral transmission were in opposing camps. The debate was, and still is, an important one, as was acknowledged by biblical scholars of the period.[10] Both folklorists and biblical scholars share a common history of dispute as to the trustworthiness of oral transmission. In fact, as will emerge, Old Testament studies have relied heavily on the findings and theories of folklore studies in order to substantiate many of the biblical claims to historicity.

2. What is Folklore?

Unfortunately the way in which the term 'folklore' has been used by biblical scholars varies—a situation which, as much as anything else, probably reflects the state of affairs within the discipline of folklore itself. Implicit in J.G. Frazer's definition of folklore are assumptions of the antiquity of the material and its collective (and therefore anonymous) character. Both these notions however, are judgments of a circumstantial rather than substantial nature. They do not provide adequate criteria for defining a particular element within the material as folklore. There are other definitions given by F.L. Utley[11] and the enumerative ones provided by W. Thoms.[12] Helpful as these definitions may be, however, they by no means command universal assent. The diversity of opinions amongst folklore scholars is best illustrated by the nineteen separate entries given under the term 'folklore' in Funk and Wagnall's dictionary of folklore.[13]

Nevertheless, despite the vast differences in definition of the term folklore, the two criteria which appear in almost all definitions are: (a) the means by which folklore is transmitted and (b) the concept of tradition. Whatever the substance of folklore, traditional or otherwise, the oral character of its transmission has always been considered integral to any definition.[14] As D. Ben-Amos has pointed out:

the oral aspect of a tradition has become amongst folklore scholars the last citadel in determining the uniqueness of their material.[15]

This aspect of orality however, only qualifies the manner by which folklore is transmitted. What is transmitted is not defined. For this we must look to the second most frequently cited definition, i.e. the concept of tradition. S. Thompson considers this to be the touchstone for anything which is to be thought of as folklore,[16] and P. Utley rightly comments that within the definitions listed in Funk and Wagnall, the concept of tradition goes unchallenged.[17]

Implied in the term tradition is that which has survived and been passed on within a community throughout many generations. As such the antiquity of the various materials is presumed, since they are considered by definition to be remaining specimens of a bygone age.

These two elements, oral transmission and traditions passed on in a community are what constitute the study of folklore. For Ben-Amos these two aspects cannot and should not be separated. The telling of a folktale and the folktale itself cannot be separated, for the tale is in its telling.[18]

J.W. Rogerson has suggested that the principal influence of folklore scholarship on Old Testament studies has been with regard to those 'theories of folklorists about traditions transmitted orally',[19] and accepts the *Oxford English Dictionary*'s definition of folklore as the study of 'traditions, beliefs and customs of the common people'.[20] In this way Rogerson does not create a false dichotomy between the mode of transmission and that which is transmitted, thereby avoiding Ben-Amos' strictures against most definitions of folklore.

However Ben-Amos' own definition of folklore completely ignores these two elements, which he regards as too limiting for the scope and content of folklore. He prefers to define folklore as 'artistic communication in small groups'.[21] By thus excluding the notion of oral transmission, Ben-Amos has attempted to broaden the normally accepted definition of folklore to include materials which would otherwise have gone unnoticed. By excluding the notion of tradition the antiquity of the material ceases to be an issue. It may be that the material is very old but it is not necessarily the case that those transmitting the material are aware of its antiquity. If a diachronic approach to folklore is undertaken, then methodologically what is essential is to be able to study both that which has survived as folklore and that which has been lost in the transmission process, if

1. Folklore Studies and Old Testament Criticism 17

only to be able to use the latter as a control group. It is precisely the lack of such a control group which makes comparative folklore research hypothetical in its findings. If we take for example J.G. Frazer's analysis of Genesis 27, there is no way of establishing what aspect of the narrative has degenerated. What might be the vestiges of an ancient rite, may also be interpreted as part of the story-teller's art.

Similarly, for Ben-Amos, the concept of oral transmission is also deficient since it is bound up with ideas of antiquity and purity. This presupposition of a pure, oral text uninfluenced by the written word has resulted in a tendency among folklorists to concentrate on obscure and unique texts, whereas, given the inevitable interchange between written and oral means of communication, folklorists should be concentrating more on the 'notion of folklore as a process'.[22] What makes a text folkloristic for Ben-Amos is not so much its history as its ongoing existence in the community.

More recently, R.M. Dorson, while recognizing that folklore studies began as a discipline which was 'past minded and past begotten, the shards and shreds, leftovers and relics of a departed age',[23] now argues that the concept of tradition should be understood as a dynamic force which is being continually updated within a community. L. Dégh and A. Vazsonyi retain 'tradition' as part of their definition of folklore not because it designates antiquity but rather because, as an entity within culture, it keeps surprisingly abreast of the times. The two meanings of tradition as 'culture passed on' and 'the procedure of passing on of culture' increasingly approximate to each other.[24]

These subtle shifts in folklorists' attempts to define their discipline not only affect their own work, but also have ramifications for biblical studies. In so far as these observations are crucial to the debate as to what constitutes folklore, it has for our purposes highlighted the two most relevant issues for biblical studies.

3. Folklore Research and its Influence on Old Testament Studies

There have been three main areas of folklore studies which have influenced approaches to Old Testament studies. The first, as we have seen, was that area of folklore studies which could be identified with the cultural anthropological approach of J.G. Frazer; secondly the generic approach as practised by the brothers Grimm and then adapted by biblical literary critics; and thirdly, and closely allied to the second (perhaps more properly to be considered as a subcategory), theories relating to oral composition and transmission most clearly outlined by A. Olrik and first overtly applied to the biblical text by H. Gunkel and the adherents of form-criticism.

The influence of folklore studies on theories relating to oral composition and transmission of biblical narrative has not always been openly acknowledged. More often than not scholars in the past have given scant recognition to a discipline which undoubtedly informed many of their presuppositions and provided them with a methodology with which to interpret the biblical text. Research has shown the influence the brothers Grimm had on twentieth-century German biblical scholarship.[25] What has yet to occur is the equal realization that folklore studies has not stood still. Many folklorists now sharply criticize the assumptions of scholars who were influenced by nineteenth-century Romanticism.[26] As I have also indicated, the definition of folklore itself has changed, as has the emphasis of the discipline—shifting from the historical search for the *Urtext* and/or custom, to a more process-oriented approach. The main concern of this book, however, is with folklore's contribution to the study of oral narratives and the influence it has had on biblical studies.

4. *The Documentary Hypothesis*

I have chosen to begin with a brief discussion of Wellhausen's literary analysis of the Pentateuch, since it was his presentation of the documentary hypothesis which formed the presuppositions of subsequent form-critical and tradition-historical analyses.

Wellhausen's conclusions concerning the formation of the Pentateuch were first worked out in a series of articles published in 1876 and 1877.[27] By employing the techniques of literary criticism, Wellhausen concluded that the Pentateuch consisted of four different sources which could be separated one from the other. By postulating the existence of four sources which were given the sigla J, E, D, and P, the various problems of the text, such as contradictions within both narrative and legal materials, diversity of style and multiple renditions of the same event, could be accounted for.

Wellhausen's unique contribution however, was his *Geschichte Israels* I,[28] where he used these methods of literary criticism to

1. Folklore Studies and Old Testament Criticism 19

reconstruct Israel's history. In it he argued that the Pentateuch contained three strata of law and three of tradition,[29] and that the problem for the historian lay in discovering their true chronological order. These strata of law and tradition themselves testified to five issues involved in worship and cultic life, i.e. the place of worship, sacrifice, sacred feasts, priests and Levites, and the endowment of the clergy. As regards each issue it could be shown that each source betrayed a particular outlook which was coterminous with different periods in Israel's history. These five issues showed an historical progression, reflected in the sources themselves, which could therefore be placed in chronological order.

Taking as his starting point the book of Deuteronomy, Wellhausen argued on the basis of 2 Kings 22-23, that Josiah's reform was the first to institute regulations declaring the legitimacy of the one sanctuary in Jerusalem and the destruction of all others. Thus, Deuteronomy belonged to the seventh century. In comparison to D, he maintained that the J and E documents relfected religious and cultic attitudes which would have existed prior to the pre-exilic prophetic movement of the mid-eighth century. Deuteronomic legislation was formulated largely as a result of this prophetic movement.[30] By comparing the material contained within P (Exod. 25-31; 35-40; Leviticus; Num. 1.1-10.10) with that of D, Wellhausen, here dependent upon Graf, concluded that P was later than D and should be regarded as the framework which gave the Pentateuch its final form at the time of the reforms of Ezra and Nehemiah.[31]

The documents themselves were combined by various redactors at different periods in Israelite history. Thus J and E were combined in the time of the Josianic reform and later added to D,[32] while P provided the final framework into which J, E, D were fitted, some time during the fifth century.

Each document betrayed a particular bias which was the result of its author's own particular *Tendenz*, and could therefore be used as evidence of the history of the period of its composition.[33] This made it exceedingly difficult, if not impossible, to differentiate between the history of the period which the source was purporting to record, and the particular author's understanding of that history. Nonetheless, Wellhausen did concede that once the historical details of the individual author's own *Tendenz* were accounted for, the fragmentary information left in the document could be used as historical evidence of the period which the source was describing. Thus, Wellhausen acknowledged that at least in some instances the origin of the documents was not necessarily identical with the origin of their content. In brief outline these were the conclusions reached by Wellhausen, conclusions which were to gain wide acceptance amongst the vast majority of biblical scholars.[34]

Although Wellhausen considered the various sources of the Pentateuch to have been written by separate authors and then combined by different redactors, he did suggest that at least some of the material in J reflected a much earlier period than that of its composition. On the one hand he stated:

> We attain to no historical knowledge of the patriarchs but only of the time when the stories about them arose in the Israelite people; this later age is here consciously projected in its inner and outward features into hoar antiquity and is reflected there like a glorified mirage.[35]

He also conceded that however much the sources betrayed a later age, some of them had their beginnings in a much earlier period of Israel's history. Oral transmission of these stories had played a part, but the history of that transmission was now lost. Furthermore, the process of transmission meant that the original story had been irretrievably altered:

> The longer a story was spread by oral tradition among the people the more was its roots concealed by the schools springing from it.[36]

From such statements it is evident that in the main Wellhausen did not have much confidence in the historical reliability of orally transmitted material. Referring to the stories contained within the J corpus in Genesis he concedes that some of the stories had a pre-literary history:

> From the mouth of the people there comes nothing but the detached narratives which may or may not happen to have some bearing on each other; to weave them together in a connected whole is the work of the poetical or literary artist.[37]

Although Wellhausen acknowledged and made reference to 'oral folklore' he went to great lengths to argue against such remnants existing in any intelligible form in Genesis. Indeed where he does discuss ideas of oral folklore or oral tradition[38] it is with reference to the P source, which he denies betrays any suggestion of having been

1. *Folklore Studies and Old Testament Criticism* 21

orally transmitted.[39] The extent of oral tradition is limited to speculation about numbers:

> Oral folklore can very well contain round numbers, such as the twelve sons and the seventy souls of the family of Jacob, the twelve wells and the seventy palm trees at Ehin...; but a chronological system, whole lists of exact and considerable numbers, bare catalogues of personal names, none of them having any significance, dates and measurements such as those in the account of the flood in the Priestly code, require writing even to originate, not to speak of transmitting them.[40]

The fact that many of the self-contained narratives within the J corpus originated in diverse localities could be seen in 'how little they have coalesced into a unity'.[41] Yet to search behind the unity imposed by the author of J, to ask questions about the pre-literary stage of the narratives, would yield nothing. The techniques of folklore composition and transmission would be of little use to the exegete. A pre-literary stage, if there had been one, was now too much affected by the written word:

> Even at the first act of reducing it to writing, the discolouring influences are at work, without any violence being done to the meaning which dwells in the matter.[42]

Any agreement there may be in the respective sources is strictly the result of literary dependence.[43]

Although Wellhausen did not attempt to trace the development of Israelite legend,[44] he nonetheless accepted that there had existed independent self-contained units which had been brought together at the written stage. What he refused to accept was the possibility of tracing the history of these units prior to their collection and writing. For Wellhausen the connection made between the legends was only secondary:

> As with the legend of the beginnings of things, so with the legend of the patriarchs: what is essential and original is the individual element in the several stories: the connection is a secondary matter, and only introduced on the stories being collected and reduced to writing.[45]

This is not to imply, however, that these individual legends originated during the period they recount. Here Wellhausen distinguished between the legends of creation, those of origin, the patriarchs, and Moses. The period of Moses and Joshua is represented by epic, and there can be no doubt that historical factors underlie the narrative:

> We should decline the historical standard in the case of the legend of the origins of mankind and of the legend of the patriarchs, while we employ it to a certain extent for the epic period of Moses and Joshua. The epic tradition certainly contains elements which cannot be explained on any other hypothesis than that there are historical facts underlying them; its source is in the period it deals with, while the patriarchal legend has no connection whatever with the times of the patriarchs.[46]

It is clear then, that apart from a general idea that there is such a thing as oral folklore and that it was probably responsible for the legends of the patriarchs, Wellhausen does not elaborate upon the subject of oral composition and transmission. He is definite that the period reflected in the patriarchal narratives is that of the period of Israel's monarchy.[47] He is also specific in describing these legends as self-contained units, utilized in narrative which itself is the creation of a 'literary artist':

> When the subject treated is not history but legends about pre-historic times, the arrangement of the materials does not come with the materials themselves, but must arise out of the plan of a narrator.[48]

The pre-literary stage of these legends is impossible to determine and therefore the history of their pre-literary forms cannot be reconstructed. The period prior to Moses is one which is now inaccessible to the historian apart from scant archaeological evidence. Folklore, then, was seen by Wellhausen as having played but a minor part in the contents of Genesis. The individual legends have been so transformed in their transcription that their oral pre-history is not lost.[49] We can recognize the presence of oral tradition by its penchant for miracles, angels, dreams, etymologies and proverbs.[50] Wellhausen did not indicate why these elements were more the hallmark of orality than literacy, however. Furthermore the qualitative difference he makes between the age of the patriarchs, and that of Moses, is arbitrary and subjective—owing, one suspects, more to theological judgments than to literary or historical ones.

In view of these and other criticisms it is not surprising that apart from those critics who either sought to discredit Wellhausen's

1. *Folklore Studies and Old Testament Criticism*

theories or to modify them, there arose a reaction amongst scholars which was far more radical. Their discontent was directed against Wellhausen's concentration on the development of the written stages of the text to the exclusion of the history of its oral composition and transmission.[51]

5. *H. Gunkel and the Form-Critical Search for an Oral Text*

The influence of folklore on form-critical method is best understood in the context of genre criticism and the work of the brothers Grimm. The impact which the research of the brothers Grimm had on folklore studies[52] was also to have far-reaching consequences for Old Testament studies.

Although the brothers Grimm were not the first to produce collections of folktales, it was their research into the field of folktale composition and transmission which was to become the basis of all future research in the area. Their first collection of German folktales appeared in the early nineteenth century in a two-volume edition entitled *Kinder- und Hausmärchen*[53] and was later followed by Jacob Grimm's *Deutsche Mythologie*.[54] Two aspects of their work influenced Old Testament studies in particular. First their definitions of various literary genres within folk narrative and second, their interest in oral transmission.

Within folklore studies much of the nineteenth century was spent debating the origins of various folktales. While folklorists such as M. Müller sought to relate the origins of all Aryan folklore to various solar mythologies by means of a complex and at times fantastic method of comparative philology, others such as A. Lang argued that primitive people everywhere had had similar beliefs and tales, which had survived in classic Greek myths and modern folklore.[55] It was the latter theory which, after Müller's death, held sway, and as we shall see, most likely informed H. Gunkel's first thinking on the origins of many of the patriarchal narratives.[56]

In an introduction to M. Hunt's translation of *Kinder- und Hausmärchen*, A. Lang stated that the roots of these folktales were to be located in Aryan mythology.[57] Myths were understood as stories about gods and included descriptions of the elemental forces and change in history. The legend or heroic epic localized the myth in actual places and attributed the adventures of the gods to various characters. What is found in the folktale is the final and youngest form of the legend. Thus the folktale lacked local habitation, drawing freely from the imagination, unlike legend which carried with it almost the authority of history. Finally, according to Lang, the folktale was used primarily as entertainment.

With such issues being the focus of debate within folklore studies, and with so much emphasis being placed on the literature of the folk, it seems strange that Wellhausen should have remained so adamantly opposed to asking questions about a possible pre-literary stage of the pentateuchal narratives. Nevertheless, the questions were posed by Gunkel, whose methods of biblical criticism were very much informed by folklore research.

Maintaining that the methods of literary criticism had led to an excessive interest in the dissection of the biblical text into more and more sources, Gunkel sought instead to trace the pre-literary stages of the narratives in Genesis back to their origins[58] He provided a method whereby the pre-literary stages of the traditions within Genesis could be studied. In *Schöpfung und Chaos in Urzeit und Endzeit*, Gunkel stated his thesis that much of the narrative material in Genesis is legend (*Sage*) and had its origins in an oral stage, long before it obtained a fixed literary form.[59] His understanding of the legend was worked out in his commentary on Genesis, which was first published in 1901.[60]

Fundamental to Gunkel's thesis was his conviction that legend should be distinguished from history writing. Whereas legend was originally part of an oral tradition, history was usually found in written form. Legend was concerned with personal family matters whereas history was mainly interested in political events which affected the state. Finally, unlike history, which is usually conveyed in prose, legend very often betrayed a certain poetic tone.[61]

Gunkel divided the book of Genesis into two parts. The first, chs. 1-11, consisted of more mythically oriented stories. The second, chs. 12-50, consisted in large part of individual legends which dealt with the lives of the patriarchs. These legends could be divided into three main groups: the historical legend which deals with migrations of tribes and the treaties they made; the ethnographic legend which in many cases, although referring to individuals, actually recounts the events of tribes; and finally there was the etiological legend which could itself be classified as ethnological, etymological, ceremonial and geological. Apart from these groups Gunkel argued that there existed legends of mixed character which could contain any number of the above types.[62]

1. Folklore Studies and Old Testament Criticism 25

Although Genesis is not written in poetry, in general it is correct to assume that the poetic form of a tradition predates the prose version. Thus it was precisely those stories of creation and the flood which were found in extra-biblical sources and known to predate the Genesis acounts which were in poetic form.[63] Genesis, should be considered a folk book, i.e. a collection of legends which had existed as popular oral tradition before being committed to writing. In this way much of the archaic language could be accounted for.[64] In addition Gunkel argued that the very structure of the legend betrayed its origins in oral composition. This structure, as outlined in the first edition of his commentary on Genesis, anticipated many of the conclusions of A. Olrik who was working in the area of folklore. In 1909 Olrik published a paper entitled 'Epische Gesetze der Volksdichtung' in which he isolated thirteen principles governing the composition of oral literature. These principles, or rather 'laws', were not restricted to one particular genre but could be applied equally to folktale, myth, legend and folksong. Thus by 1910, when the third edition of Gunkel's commentary was published, many of his conclusions received added authority from the results of A. Olrik.[65]

The extent of the agreement between these two men can be seen when we compare their results.[66] For both, the *Sage*:[67] (1) could be seen as having a distinct introduction and conclusion;[68] (2) frequently contained repetitive elements in order to intensify interest;[69] (3) had a small number of characters;[70] (4) related the actions of only a few characters in any given scene since the listener would not be able to cope with a vast diversity;[71] (5) had a very clear and simple narrative framework whose story did not attempt to fill in prerequisite data;[72] (6) reflected rigid patterning;[73] (7) had a clear unity of plot;[74] and (8) focused on one personage, with the result that:

> The hearer does not have to ask many questions to learn which of the personages should receive his special attention.[75]

Gunkel's findings thus received almost unconditional support from Olrik. Not only was the basic form and structure of the *Sage* in general and the legend in particular defined, but Gunkel now had evidence from the field of folklore that such criteria reflected oral composition. (How far we can rely on Olrik's 'epic laws' will be discussed in Chapter 2.)

Having identified the legend's form and structure Gunkel went on to postulate a typical *Sitz im Leben* for this particular genre. The legend would have been narrated by members of a class of professional story-tellers who would have practised their art around the camp-fire and at popular festivals.[76] The actual origin of the patriarchal narratives was a different matter and Gunkel's thinking on the issue shifted, so that by the time of the third edition of his Genesis commentary he no longer considered the legends to have derived from more ancient myths. Now Gunkel was prepared to accept the arguments of H. Gressmann[77] (himself dependent upon the thinking of W. Wundt[78]) that the patriarchal legends derived from more ancient folktales (*Märchen*).[79] The patriarchal narratives did not have their origins in Canaanite mythology, nor were the patriarchs 'demoted gods'.[80] Rather, these patriarchal narratives were derived from folktales and were of old Hebrew origin.[81] The stories about the patriarchs had originally been about the lives of individual shepherds, and were not the residual characters of ancient myth.[82]

Having established the original 'oral' form of the patriarchal narratives and located their origin in ancient folktales, Gunkel proceeded to identify various folktale motifs which were to be found within the Old Testament. In 1917 he published a work in which he sought to compare various Old Testament materials with folktales from all over the world.[83] This study was an attempt to uncover the earliest forms of Old Testament literature. If the folktale was the original form of the legend and if various folktale motifs could be isolated, then that original form could be identified.

The results of this comparison seemed to substantiate Gunkel's claim that beneath much of the Old Testament there remained a residue of older tradition which had originated in folktales. In so far as these folktale motifs existed, they betrayed or reflected a primitive mentality which personified the natural world. They were primarily interested in magic, and focused their attention on demons, giants and witches.

The methodological problems with this approach are obvious. It is highly doubtful whether a transcultural analysis of this kind can result in valid conclusions about the 'primitive' beliefs of the ancient Hebrews. Furthermore, personification is not always the result of a 'primitive' mind; it can be, and often is, the creation of a highly sophisticated form of poetics. However, this conception of what constituted the primitive mentality is one which informed Gunkel's understanding of the world in which the legend was told, and reflects

1. *Folklore Studies and Old Testament Criticism*   27

many anthropological presuppositions which informed the folklorists of his day.

On the basis of the information contained within the legends of Genesis, Gunkel proceeded to reconstruct a primitive form of society together with the mentality of its people. These ancient story-tellers were to be admired for their simplicity. While the world which the legend depicted was not identical with the world of the ancient story tellers, it nonetheless reflected a stage of narrative art which was less sophisticated than even the legends found in the books of Samuel. No doubt it was the romantic concept of 'primitive man', prevalent in the nineteenth century, which influenced much of Gunkel's thinking.

Central to this romantic approach to 'folk' literature was the idea that it reflected an artless spontaneity, which sprang from the depths of primitive man's consciousness. Connected with this idea was a particular understanding of tradition. In so far as such 'primitive' literature was the result of unconscious and unprompted actions, so its preservation from one generation to the next was equally unconscious. The notion of the 'collective' consciousness, or, perhaps more strictly speaking, 'unconsciousness' of 'primitive' man, was thus given great emphasis:

> The feeling that through folk popular art one could reach back to the lost period of natural spontaneous literary utterance as well as to the deep and natural springs of national identity was basic to the romantic attitude, and received extra force through ideological and nationalist references to tradition.[84]

The belief grew that by studying folklore material it was possible to recover in the oral traditions of a society what that society had at one time believed, and how the society had been structured—hence J.G. Frazer's belief that folklore constituted 'the collective action of the multitude'.[85]

In addition to romantic ideas of the spontaneous, untrained and collective nature of oral literature, there persists the notion of a special 'folk memory', capable of faithfully preserving traditions over a long period of time.[86] This 'traditional' quality of folklore was, and in many ways still is, considered to be an incontrovertible truth.

It is these assumptions about oral literature, i.e. that it was a product of a spontaneous mind, a reflection of communal experience, and traditional in so far as it was faithfully transmitted from one generation to the next, which were prevalent in folklore studies during Gunkel's day, and to a large extent still prevail:

> Writers on various forms of oral literature constantly make direct and indirect reference to the supposed 'homogeneous', 'unsophisticated', 'communal', 'co-operative', characteristics of the sort of culture where oral tradition or folk-art 'must have' existed or 'would naturally' or actually 'did' thrive.[87]

How far then did Gunkel's conception of 'primitive' man reflect these aspects of general folklore theory? It is evident from much of Gunkel's writing that his own conceptions of 'primitive man' reflected the same bias as that found within folklore studies. Firstly, Gunkel postulated that legends had been the creation of individual composers, whose interests and concerns reflected a certain spontaneity in so far as they were the outcome of men's everyday experience. They began as an unconscious art form.[88] The stories they told were simple and uncomplicated, since 'men of antiquity were in general more simple than many-sided men of modern times'.[89] Secondly, these short compositions although originating from individual composers, were nonetheless produced by the whole of the people. They were the result of the people's mind.[90] The legend was part of traditional lore in so far as it had been transmitted orally from generation to generation, resulting in a 'class of professional story-tellers familiar with old songs and legends' (who) 'wandered about the country, and were probably to be found regularly at the popular festivals'.[91] Apart from these three particular aspects of primitive man, Gunkel included the following observations:

a. Both the narrator and the audience assumed legends to be historically true because they: 'Come from ages and stages of civilization which have not yet acquired the intellectual power to distinguish between poetry and reality'.[92]
b. The primitive artist may not have known how to 'reflect' but this was compensated for by his ability to observe.[93]
c. Primitive man preferred short narrative productions and this was a sign of the relative age of a legend: 'The briefer a saga, the greater the probability, that we have it in its original form'.[94]

The proposition that the primitive mind had a limited concentration span and would therefore have only understood legends of short duration is itself a simplistic notion and one which can no longer be upheld. Indeed it is questionable whether Gunkel ever had other

1. Folklore Studies and Old Testament Criticism

than 'Rousseauesque' reasons for maintaining such an argument. It does however reveal an important aspect of Gunkel's theories of oral composition and transmission, i.e. that regardless of the non-historical content of legend it was possible to isolate the oldest parts of Genesis by locating its shortest, self-contained units.[95] In so doing the historian could gain valuable information, which could help in the reconstruction of former historical periods. It is evident that Gunkel's anthropological presuppositions, which he shared with the folklorists of his day, informed many of his assumption concerning the form and content of oral composition.

Neither should the importance of Gunkel's postulated story-tellers be underestimated, for this aspect of his theory acts as the basis for his understanding of how the legends were transmitted from generation to generation. These same story-tellers were responsible for taking the individual legends and joining them with others to form legend cycles (*Sagenkränze*).[96] The primary device used in forming these legend cycles was the journey motif which acted as a link beteen the individual legends.[97] The second device used to combine individual legends was that of the framework story (*Rahmerzählung*).[98] This is clearly illustrated by the Esau/Jacob legends which act as a frame for the Jacob/Laban cycle.[99] Although the legends contained within a cycle were frequently about one particular character, they nonetheless contained references to many different geographical localities. Gunkel argued that this was as a result of the story-tellers moving from one location to another and changing details of the story accordingly.[100] Consequently it was impossible to establish the original location of each one of the patriarchs.[101] Notwithstanding this, Gunkel still asserted with confidence that the process of bringing together the patriarchal legends took place long before the Israelites migrated into Canaan, even though it was probably during the period of the monarchy that the greatest impetus for amalgamation occurred.[102]

Gunkel was not always consistent in his argument for the reliability of oral transmission. Likening an ancient audience to children who reproach a story-teller for making a mistake or creating a variant, Gunkel argued for the fidelity of the transmission process.[103] Even so, he admitted that the legend could not remain totally unchanged:

> the popular legend cannot permanently remain the same...

> Slowly and hesitatingly, always at a certain distance behind, the legends follow the general changes in conditions, some more some less.[104]

This very process of change within legends provides us with a means of charting the cultural changes which the people of ancient Israel had gone through. So for Gunkel there remained both a stable and a variable element in the history of the transmission of the legend. By careful and sensitive analysis the historian might be able to trace its lines of development.[105] The process of transmission, however, does not only involve accretions, it also entails the loss of certain vital information. Consequently,

> There is spread over many legends something like a blue haze which veils the colours of the landscape.[106]

The process of transmission is thus complex. For even though there remain ancient features in the narratives which can be identified, these have been enveloped by later narratives which have added new elements and shed certain old ones. Oral tradition was therefore one which had preserved many ancient legends but had also forgotten many others—the legends about sanctuaries being the least well preserved. Lapse of memory, however, is more than made up for by the imagination 'which is mightily stirred by such narratives, (and) develops them involuntarily'.[107] It is as a consequence of these modifications that the legends can provide evidence for the history of Israelite religion.[108]

After c. 1200 BC no new patriarchal stories were composed, and the legends began to become fixed oral tradition until c. 900 BC, when they achieved the form preserved in the written text.[109] The collection of these legends into cycles and the joining together of legend cycles began at the oral stage. Those who wrote these legends down were never more than collectors and were only responsible for some slight alterations. With the gradual disappearance of professional story-tellers there arose a need for the transcription of these legends.[110] Nonetheless, the collection process had already begun at the oral stage, and the first written versions were of connected narratives. '"J" and "E" then, are not individual authors nor are they editors of older and consistent writings, but rather they are schools of narrators.'[111] However faithful the collectors were in preserving the original details of these legends, Gunkel argued that the collecting

1. *Folklore Studies and Old Testament Criticism* 31

and editing processes had resulted in an alteration in the impression made by the legends:

> In general we are disposed to say that the oral tradition is responsible for a certain artistic inner modification, and the collectors for a more superficial alteration consisting merely of omissions and additions.[112]

Gunkel's acknowledgment that the process of collection is as complicated as the process of oral transmission allows him considerable room for manoeuvre in his reconstruction. Maintaining both conservatism and change in oral transmission allows him to chart a literary history of J and E—one which stretches from c. 1500 BC to the first half of the eighth century, after which a redactor, the Jehovist, joined the two sources some time near the end of the kingdom of Judah.[113] The most salient point to note is that Gunkel postulated a period of some 600 years of oral transmission, a period which saw the transformation of various legends, but nonetheless one which preserved a wealth of ancient narrative.

Gunkel's theories of oral composition and transmission of the Genesis legends are lucidly laid out in an article which he published in 1919 on Jacob.[114] Here the implication of his acceptance of the folktale as the basis of the individual legend are fully spelled out. Gunkel argued that the original component of the Jacob cycle was to be found in the Jacob and Esau stories of the sale of the birthright and the deception over the blessing.[115] This unit had originally been a folktale about a shepherd and a hunter.[116] The other unit predating the cycle had been the Jacob/Laban story, which was originally a folktale telling of a contest between an older and a younger shepherd.[117]

In the original form of the story Jacob and Laban are not related, but in order to connect the Jacob/Esau story with the Jacob/Laban story, the kinship theme is supplied. Thus, Jacob's going to Laban, his uncle, on the advice of his mother (Gen. 27.42-45) provides, on the basis of the 'journey motif', the means by which the two stories are connected.[118] The second part of the Esau story (Gen. 32.1-33) is a free composition of the story-teller, the main connecting motif being Jacob's cunning.[119] In so far as the patriarchal narratives were originally folktales and only subsequently obtained historical connections, so too were the patriarchs themselves originally folktale characters, who only subsequently became nationalized as eponymous figures.[120] Jacob and Esau are not a reflection of the historical situation which obtained between Israel and Edom during the patriarchal period. Rather, Gunkel argued, the period reflected was that of the Davidic monarchy. David's subjugation of the Edomites provides a situation in which the story of Jacob's birthright and blessing could be interpreted nationally.[121] Laban the Aramean acquired his eponymous status only after the Aramean wars,[122] during the early monarchy when Israel was first emerging as a unified state.[123] Most important for Gunkel's argument was his contention that various cultic sanctuaries only became connected with Jacob once he had become a national figure.[124] Therefore the cultic aetiologies were subsequent additions to the patriarchal narratives and not integral to them.[125] Finally, Gunkel maintained that the only element of tribal history found in the narratives was that regarding the birth of Jacob's sons.[126]

This study of the Jacob cycle was Gunkel's final attempt to systematize a programme of *Literaturgeschichte* for the legends in Genesis. Unlike Wellhausen who had maintained that the oral stage could not be uncovered, Gunkel sought to establish criteria by which the earliest form of the tradition could be detected. Not only had the original forms of the legends been composed orally, but their subsequent collection into cycles had also taken place at the oral stage. The earliest form of the tradition was contained in a folktale, (probably reaching back as far as 1500 BC) around which later material was attached. Indeed, with the exception of the two folktales, all other material originated after 980 BC. Unlike Wellhausen, Gunkel believed that those responsible for the J and E documents were not literary authors but rather collectors and records of a previously fixed oral tradition. thus what Wellhausen presumed could only be the result of a literary activity, Gunkel argued was the product of a professional class of story-tellers.

As I have attempted to show, Gunkel's genre classification of legend is radically changed in his later work. Ethnographic and cultic aetiologies which had previously been thought to lie at the heart of the genre, he later considered to be secondary developments. The patriarchal legends were now understood as having derived from older folktales, not myths, and the patriarchs were seen as having emerged out of folktale characters. At a later stage these characters became eponymous figures and the narratives then functioned as ethnographic aetiologies. Only after this stage are cultic aetiologies associated with the eponymous figures. As a genre, therefore, the legend began as a folktale, its sole purpose being one of entertainment. Its subsequent development is reflected in its acquisition (while still at the oral stage) first of ethnological and then cultic aetiologies.[127] Gunkel, therefore, arrived at the following conclusions:

1. The major part of Genesis 12–50 consists of legends. Following Gressmann's use of Wundt, Gunkel argued that the legend derived from folktale, and not myth as had previously been maintained by the brothers Grimm. The oldest legends were originally folktales, which were composed by a professional class of story-tellers for the purpose of entertainment. Gradually these tales accumulated ethnological and cultic aetiologies.
2. These legends were originally oral. The criteria for establishing the original oral composition of a narrative were substantiated by the findings of Olrik working in the area of folklore studies. For the first time a set of 'laws' governing oral composition was promulgated.
3. The antiquity of these legends was attested by their simplicity and brevity. Only a primitive society could have composed and transmitted such legends, since by definition they were unsophisticated. The discipline of folklore maintained that remnants of such societies could still be detected in the written accounts of their oral traditions.
4. The main vehicle of legend transmission was a professional class of story-tellers. After 1200 BC no new patriarchal legends were composed. From this time until 900 BC the legends were collected together to form cycles concerning certain individual patriarchs. These legends were transmitted with great fidelity, yet as collectors of folklore had demonstrated, degeneration also occurred due to faulty memory, leaving only residual traces of a bygone age.
5. Because of the process of degeneration, the patriarchal stories could not be used as historical narrative. Nonetheless, there were portions of the narrative which betrayed great antiquity and which could therefore shed light on the sociological setting of the period 1500–900 BC.

It is evident, then, that folklore studies influenced Old Testament research in its understanding of oral narrative composition, and the mechanisms of oral narrative transmission. Both these areas have played significant and influential roles in our understanding of how the ancient Israelites interpreted their world. Once such theories of oral narrative composition and transmission became discredited among folklorists, however, inevitably their application to the study of the Old Testament must be brought into question.

6. *Tradition-Historical Approaches and the Assumption of Faithful Transmission*

Gunkel's approach to the legends of Genesis was similar to that of an archaeologist to a tell. He assumed that the different layers of the text could be stripped off until eventually the oldest unit was revealed.

Two major objections to this approach were raised by subsequent scholars. The first objection involved the recognition that as a document J displayed a unity which betrayed a common theological outlook. It would therefore seem more likely that the collecting and arranging of initially independent units was the act of an author(s) rather than of a school of legend collectors. The second major objection to Gunkel's approach came from various Scandinavian scholars who maintained that the very process of oral transmission obscured the stages through which the material passed, making it impossible to reconstruct a history of the literature.

In either case, since these objections deal with the traditions[128] of Genesis at the pre-literary stage and their contribution to the field of oral narrative composition and transmission, they will both be discussed under the one heading, tradition-historical approaches.[129]

a. *A. Alt*

A. Alt's contribution to the study of the patriarchs is contained in his 1919 essay on patriarchal religion.[130] His thesis, that the religion of the pre-settlement period had been based on the worship of a 'God of the fathers' cult, influenced both G. von Rad and M. Noth. Following Gunkel, Alt accepted that the original unit of the patriarchal narrative was the legend (*Sage*) and that the simple form of the legend could be separated out from its secondary complex. By establishing the ancient form of the legend it was theoretically possible to discover aspects of an earlier religion which had hitherto remained hidden.[131] If careful attention was paid to the patriarchal

1. Folklore Studies and Old Testament Criticism 35

legends the unique religious element practised by individual tribes could be identified—and that element was the tradition of the God of the fathers.[132] Alt proposed that the patriarchal association with cult sanctuaries was not a literary creation. The cult of the fathers had originated amongst the semi-nomadic tribes who eventually migrated into Canaan during the settlement period. The cults and the names of their founders (Abraham, Isaac, Jacob) were transferred to the various sanctuaries which were already established in the land. The biblical tradition had not preserved any legends of the actual founding of the cults because this occurred prior to the entry into Canaan.[133] Once in the land the patriarchs became associated with the sanctuaries, and the earlier aetiological legends of the cults were no longer relevant. To substantiate their claim to the Palestinian sanctuaries, the traditions attribute the revelation granted to the patriarchs to the 'El' numina, previously worshipped at their shrines.[134] The oldest part of the tradition contained references to these El, numina but they were few and almost completely obscured in comparison with the tradition of the God of the Fathers. Each patriarch came to be associated with a different cult centre; Jacob and his god in the areas inhabited by the house of Joseph; Isaac in Beersheba, and Abraham at Mamre. Whereas originally all three sanctuaries would have had separate groups of worshippers attached to them, gradually these groups interacted with one another until eventually the ultimate fusion of the gods of Abraham, Isaac and Jacob into one figure, the God of the Fathers, occurred. Originally there had been other cults than those represented by the biblical tradition. But, with the exception of the cult of the 'god of Nahor', to which there remained but one reference, all traces of the others had disappeared.[135]

In this way the arrangement of the legends in Genesis could be explained as a coherent reflection of 'organic growth' and not merely as a loose conglomeration of disparate material. The universal and exclusive worship of Yahweh did not occur immediately but was a gradual process. It included a period during which the worship of Yahweh existed alongside that of the tribal cults, until eventually the former took over the dominant position. These stages of development were all present in the text, and, by appealing to Nabatean parallels, Alt maintained that it was possible to identify the stratum which had its origins in ancient tribal religion.

Alt's general proposition has been criticized by J. Van Seters.[136] To his reservations I would add the following criticisms, which are particularly pertinent to Alt's methodology. Alt accepted with Gunkel that the oldest element of the tradition in Genesis is the individual legend. Having accepted this theoretical proposition in general, he then proceeded to ignore it when he came to the narratives which contained references to the God of the Fathers. Alt readily admitted that these references, unlike those which speak of the El numina, were more dominant in the narrative, and appeared to come from a later period. Nonetheless, he argued that they were already present in the more ancient pre-literary stage. The Yahwist, considering this portion of the tradition to be very important, brought it to the fore and elaborated the material:

> The theory and language peculiar to the Yahwist scarcely conceal the older strata that lie behind them in which the God of the Fathers is clearly visible as a distinct figure. We are more than ever forced to the conclusion that this figure was not created by the Yahwist himself, but must have had a place in the pre-literary tradition.[137]

The very principle which allowed Alt to attempt to reconstruct an older stratum of the tradition, i.e. that the oldest part is found in the individual legend, is one which he contradicted in his analysis of that tradition. The inconsistency of this approach is evident.

Regardless of these criticisms, it was Alt's insistence upon the cult as the primary institution responsible for maintaining Israel's pre-literary traditions which was to become most influential, especially on the work of von Rad and Noth.

b. *G. von Rad and M. Noth*

While von Rad was primarily concerned with understanding the basic theme of the Hexateuch, he nonetheless established new insights into its literary and oral pre-history.[138] In his monograph, *Das formgeschichtliche Problem des Hexateuch*,[139] von Rad laid the foundation for all his subsequent work on the traditions contained in the Hexateuch. Here his main concern was to establish the manner by which the Hexateuch was composed, in an attempt to identify its earliest stages of development.[140] Von Rad argued that the framework of the Hexateuch was to be found in certain confessional creeds which encapsulated Israel's faith. These creeds were found in Deut. 26.5b-9, Deut. 6.20-24, and Joshua 24. The earliest form, Deut. 26.5b-9, had probably been used by the cultic community as a

1. *Folklore Studies and Old Testament Criticism* 37

confession of faith in the God who had chosen their forefathers, liberated them from Egypt and led them to a promised land. The creed was much older than the literary form in which we find it—a form which the Deuteronomist simply records.[141] All three credal statements contained the three major tradition complexes found within the Hexateuch: the promise to the patriarchs, the exodus, and the settlement traditions.[142] Both the traditions of Genesis 1-11 and the Sinai tradition wre missing from these credal statements. Von Rad maintained that the Sinai tradition had been originally independent of the patriarchal, exodus, and occupation traditions, and only combined with them at a very late date.[143] He concluded that there had existed two separate groups of traditions which had been transmitted independently of each other: (a) the exodus and occupation tradition and (b) the Sinai tradition.[144] These two traditions had different histories, rooted in two separate cultic celebrations. The Sinai tradition was an old cult legend concerning the covenant renewal ceremony held at the feast of Booths at Shechem.[145] The exodus and occupation traditions were older than the Sinai tradition and have as their basic form the credal statement of Deut. 26.5b-9. The Sinai and settlement traditions were both cult legends. The Sinai tradition was a cult legend of the feast of Booths and the occupation tradition was a cult legend of the feast of Weeks. Once these traditions became separated from their cultic milieu, the Yahwist collected them and placed them within a literary context.[146]

Using the exodus and occupation traditions as the basic framework, the Yahwist incorporated the Sinai tradition between the two. He extended the patriarchal traditions, elaborating the old concepts of the God of the Fathers and the land promise by including various legends which he composed himself. Finally von Rad argued that the Yahwist added the primeval history in Genesis 2-11 to form a prologue.[147]

As far as the oral stage was concerned, at the heart of von Rad's thesis was the proposal that during various cultic celebrations the tradition complexes were remembered and repeated in their earliest form by the recitation of certain credal formulae. For von Rad (as for Alt), many of the patriarchal narratives which were collated by the Yahwist had originally travelled with Israel's semi-nomadic ancestors and had become attached to different sanctuaries.[148] It was, however, impossible to use these narratives as ancestral biography. The narratives could only give a few impressions of some of the cultural characteristics of the period they portrayed. Whereas the narratives gave no date for the patriarchs, von Rad, writing in his 1972 commentary on Genesis, still maintained that the environment these narratives portrayed was one of great antiquity:

> The living conditions of these semi-nomadic groups remained the same for hundreds of years, and they never made history. If one assumes (with J. Bright) that they lived early in the second millennium, then something like nine hundred years lay between them and the narratives of the Yahwist.[149]

Von Rad's appreciation of the great antiquity of much of the material contained within the patriarchal narratives was, on the whole, inherited from Gunkel. Recalling that Old Testament scholars had been designating the traditions within Genesis 'legends', von Rad credits Gunkel with having been the first scholar successfully to separate out the individual traditions from the overall narrative:

> It is to the undying credit of H. Gunkel that in his great commentary on Genesis he separated the original narrative units from the larger whole and analyzed them with a distinctive aesthetic charisma. These individual traditions were of very different kinds... a number of them were cultic aetiological narratives... some narratives are like short novelistic poems ... we are speaking now of the oldest pre-literary form of these single traditions! But that these very old traditions are for the most part 'sagas' is a fact, the background of which we can investigate no further.[150]

In so far as the narratives were legends they were concerned with history, understood as *Geschichte* rather than *Historie*. Chastising J.L.C. Grimm for his dictionary's definition of *Sage*, von Rad quoted A. Jolles to indicate the extent of the prejudice against the term *Sage*,[151] which too often became associated with fantasy. Nevertheless, the legends' particular view of history was a reflection of a pre-state society. It was the product of instinct and intuition and, unlike history writing, expressed:

> a view and interpretation not only of that which once was, but of a past event that is secretly present and decisive for the present.[152]

According to von Rad the subject matter of the legend, unlike history writing, had unmistakable qualities which allowed it to portray the past of the patriarchs in its complexity. It still retained a certain

1. Folklore Studies and Old Testament Criticism 39

religious mood, characteristic of the pre-Mosaic period. The legend, unlike 'more exact' forms preserves the private experiences of a people's past:

> The prerogative of the saga over all 'more exact' traditions is just to preserve these imponderable intimate experiences from a people's youth.[153]

The legend often described 'an entire world of events—actual experienced events—enclosed in a single legend'.[154] It was an art form which rarely indulged in expressing the emotions of its characters, and when it did, it seemed even more primitive because this occurred so rarely. The power and the influence of the legend therefore should not be underestimated:

> This is also expressed in the style. Through centuries of being told and heard, that primitive are, which can speak simply of small as well as quite important things without diminishing their substance, grew equal to the task of describing all human experience.[155]

That the legend was rooted in the environment of the family was a sign of its antiquity.[156] The long transmission of legends meant that various traditions had been expanded, sometimes by folktale motifs (*Märchenmotive*). Yet this had not affected the historical basis of the experience. We are not dealing with an imaginative construct:

> That does not mean of course that these figures and the traditions about them are nothing more than the subsequent projections of popular faith back into the primeval period. It means, rather, that this material did not lie in the archives untouched but was molded and substantially enlarged by being handed down for centuries.[157]

In general the main impetus or influence which went into forming the legend was faith, a characteristic sign of all the biblical legends. Indeed it was another sure sign of a legend's antiquity: 'The later the version of a saga, the more theologically reflective and less naive it is'.[158] The requisitioning of ancient legends by a religious tradition changed the very essence of a previously profane story. In the light of this von Rad suggested that the term 'legend' is probably an inappropriate one for the patriarchal stories. As they have come down to us, these narratives have reached a high standard of literary and theological sophistication. Although critical of the term legend, von Rad offers no alternative.

When finally these narratives were written down the Yahwist did not go beyond minor alterations of the individual legends.[159] Yet the characteristic stamp of the Yahwist is unmistakable in the way he has chosen to link together the traditions. For von Rad, Gunkel's conclusions with regard to the legends at their pre-literary stage was still an open question. In general, the exegete's task was to try to understand the text in its present form. In particular, and with reference to the patriarchal narratives, von Rad maintained that the Yahwist's 'moulding' of the transmitted material was decisive in achieving its present theological perspective.

The narratives are anchored in history in so far as they are theological interpretations of a nation's historical relationship with its God. The events behind the narrative may no longer be open to historical investigation, but the historical experience the narrative recounts was 'for the community, very much historical'.[160] This does not mean that the exegete should think of the narratives as merely an allegorical interpretation of a community's faith experience, for they contain elements of the historical.

This summary of von Rad's understanding of legend is necessary if we are to appreciate the assumptions which underlie his theory of credal formulae. While on the one hand von Rad claimed that the patriarchal narratives in their present form reflected a theological bias which made it almost impossible to discover their 'original' meaning, he insisted, on the other hand, upon retaining a belief in a historical kernel underlying all the narratives. The assumption of a historical kernel is absolutely essential, for it allows von Rad to seek out various 'historical' occurrences within the patriarchal narratives to which his credal formulae refer.

Unlike Gunkel, who maintained that many of the most ancient patriarchal narratives originated around the camp-fire, where they functioned as entertainment, von Rad accepted Jolles' conclusions as to the origins of the legend, i.e. the earliest form of the legend was the family legend which concerned itself with the telling of familial events. C. Westermann is also indebted to the work of Jolles for establishing the antiquity of the tales. Recently, Westermann in his commentary on Genesis has again relied on the thinking of Jolles. However, the theories of Jolles have not found sufficient acceptance amongst folklorists to warrant such dependence.[161] Von Rad's and Westermann's recourse to Jolles' 'family mentality', moreover, is as dubious as Gunkel's 'primitive herdsman mentality' which it claims

1. Folklore Studies and Old Testament Criticism

to supersede. Finally, the manner by which these individual narrative units in Genesis were transmitted is never elucidated by von Rad, except in so far as he argued that some of the traditions were associated with different cultic celebrations during the pre-monarchic period. It was during these festivities that the credal formulations of Deut. 25.5b-9; 6.20-24; Josh. 24.2b-13 would have been recited, and the stories would have been told during the settlement period by members of the different tribes. But given the present form of the patriarchal narratives, how are we to distinguish those tales which were originally oral from those which were the literary creation of the Yahwist? Although von Rad discussed the form and content of legend, he remained vague when discussing it as the vehicle of transmitting historical events. Recently, the possible deuteronomic origin of these credal statements has seriously undermined von Rad's theory of the composition of the Hexateuch.[162] Von Rad's major concern was with the final form of the text, since he stressed the theological influence exercised by the documentary authors over their material. Nevertheless, he maintained the existence of a period of oral composition and transmission, which may have extended over 900 years. Gunkel's theory of oral composition is still discernible, therefore, in von Rad's thinking, even though it has more recently been affected by the premises of A. Jolles.

Unlike von Rad, who had placed the emphasis on the active role of the Yahwist in his treatment of the tradition he received, Noth's thesis held that the formative period for pentateuchal traditions had been at the pre-literary stage. Whereas von Rad had traced the pre-literary stage of many of the hexateuchal traditions back to the cult, and focused much of his attention on credal formulae, Noth's main interest lay in certain themes contained within the Pentateuch and with their development. Like von Rad, Noth, in his *Überlieferungsgeschichte des Pentateuch*,[163] argued for the existence of certain faith statements which were rooted in the cult.[164] These faith statements contained basic themes which, in order of priority, included: (1) guidance out of Egypt;[165] (2) guidance into the arable land;[166] (3) promise to the patriarchs;[167] (4) guidance in the wilderness;[168] and (5) revelation at Sinai.[169] Noth concluded that these:

> Pentateuchal themes arose on the soil of the cultic life, as contents of confessions of faith which used to be recited in more or less fixed form on particular recurring cultic occasions.[170]

Each theme contained at least a kernel of historical truth and arose from the experience of the pre-Israelite tribes.[171] Only with the formation of a twelve-tribe league or amphictyony did these themes attain an all-Israel orientation. The first theme, guidance out of Egypt, came about very gradually. Those who had experienced the exodus returned and settled with other tribes in the land.[172] The story which these individuals told was then picked up by all the tribes and transmitted to successive generations as having happened to all the tribes. Gradually the remaining four themes were given an all Israel orientation. In the pre-monarchical period they were combined to form the original pentateuchal narrative which Noth signified as 'G' (*Grundlage*). Noth suggested that G, which could have been either oral or written, formed the basis of the later J and E documents, and that this accounted for their similarities.[173]

This summary of Noth's thesis can only hint at its complexities and does scant justice to the genius involved in his anlaysis. My particular concern, however, is not so much with the detailed method by which he traced the development of pentateuchal traditions as a whole, as with the part oral tradition played in his reconstruction.

It has already been shown that Noth followed von Rad in assuming an original cultic setting for the traditions of the Pentateuch. For Noth the subsequent elaboration of these traditions was a result of constant telling and retelling.[174] These expansions were founded on a huge variety of individual traditions and tradition complexes which seemed to belong to one or the other theme.[175] Although Noth stated that he was not concerned with the manner and history of the art of narration but rather with the tradition-historical aspect of the formation of the pentateuchal narrative,[176] he nonetheless maintained that there were certain themes and motifs which expert story-tellers[177] used to fill out the basic five themes of the Pentateuch:

> The Pentateuchal narrative ... grew and developed through a process of living oral transmission ... (and) contains many such general narrative schemes and motifs which are not only widely distributed but are also as old as man's practice of narration and the art of story-telling itself.[178]

For Noth these themes did not remain cultically rooted but passed from the 'mouth of the priests or the worshipping community into the mouths of popular narrators'.[179] Although the traditions were only given literary fixation at the formation of the Israelite state, they had already reached a very advanced form at the oral stage. The literary versions gave 'definite fixation to the text, in terms of their own speech and idiom and gave expression to a particular way of thinking'.[180] It was the amphictyonic community that was responsible for the collecting and combining of individual traditions. The formation of the traditions had occurred at an earlier oral stage. Whereas their substance did not alter, in the process of literary transcription changes in usage and style inevitably took place. Yet modifications in substance and disposition were far less than one might suppose, and traces of the original oral elements which form the basis of the narratives had not been obliterated.[181] Following Jolles, Noth argued that legend traditions (*Sagenüberlieferung*) flourished during the pre-state period. Once the state was established history writing replaced legend as the operative mode of expressing the past.[182] The essential difference between the two forms was that history writing was always the product of an individual, whereas the legend was the product of the whole community. In his assumptions concerning the theme of 'Promise to the Patriarchs', Noth is dependent on Alt's 'God of the Fathers' thesis. The promise of the possession of the land, originally given to the fathers when they were outside Canaan, was now seen to be fulfilled. This particular theme grew in importance and finally became associated with the other pentateuchal themes.[183] This, however, led to the notion of fulfilment becoming detached from the patriarchal narratives and associated with the theme of 'guidance into the arable land'.

The process whereby the theme of promise was incorporated into the Pentateuch was seen by Noth to be a complicated one. On the basis of von Rad's credal confessions in Deut. 26.5-9, he asssumed that the oldest part of the theme of 'promise to the patriarchs' was that relating to Jacob. Since Jacob became the ancestor of the twelve tribes and was in Egypt, he became connected with the other pentateuchal themes. At a later stage the other patriarchs were associated with these themes through Jacob.

Noth remained vague as to the date of the composition of the Jacob narratives and their incorporation into the Pentateuch. He also did not discuss how far they would have been expanded once within the Pentateuch. What is certain is that the main elements of the Jacob narrative would have become fixed before they were attached to the pentateuchal tradition at the oral stage. In contrast to the Jacob narratives, the Joseph story was considered by Noth to be later because it was not mentioned in Deut. 26.5b-9 and because of Gunkel's stricture that the more discursive style of the story betrayed its later date.[184] On the basis of Alt's 'God of the Fathers', von Rad's credal formulae, and Gunkel's theories regarding the earliest forms of oral tradition, Noth was able to maintain that the promise of land and posterity was integral to the Jacob narrative.[185]

Von Rad and Noth provide no new insights for distinguishing oral from written tradition. Whereas von Rad attributed a great deal of literary creativity to the Yahwist, Noth maintained that the formative period for the traditions remained at the oral stage. Both men accepted Gunkel's conclusions concerning the form of the earliest oral tradition units. However, both rejected the conclusion that the patriarchs were originally folklore figures, in favour of Alt's theory that they were the founders of various cult sanctuaries. For von Rad the oral tradition developed around the ancient credal statement. For Noth the themes of the credal statements developed (again at the oral stage) independently of one another, although in a definite sequence. Both von Rad and Noth held to the view that the legend material was transmitted by tribal narrators whose skills would have been much in demand during various cultic celebrations.[186] Unlike von Rad, who considered the Yahwist to have exerted a decisive influence on the final shape of the text, for Noth this influence was to be attributed to the amphictyonic community, which gave to the themes an all-Israel orientation.

Neither von Rad nor Noth considered the patriarchal narratives as historical. They retained certain historical reminiscences, which formed the kernel around which tribal narrators had added their own stories. Unlike Gunkel neither scholar saw the origins of the narratives in the folktale. Both von Rad and Noth were dependent on Jolles for their understanding of genre development.

Noth's reliance on the institution of the amphictyony for transmitting and developing the pentateuchal themes was essential if he was to maintain their all-Israelite orientation. Recently, however, the legitimacy of using such a construct has fallen into disrepute.[187] Without such a highly structured institution it is hard to see how the pentateuchal themes could have developed in such a complex way at the oral stage as Noth has suggested.

c. *Folklore and the* Urtext

The extent to which folklore studies during this period influenced the

1. *Folklore Studies and Old Testament Criticism* 45

theories of Old Testament scholars in the field of oral transmission is impossible to ascertain. Whereas the works of Olrik and Jolles had some impact upon their concepts of oral compositions, no such claim can be made for theories of oral transmission.

To a large extent, folklorists from the 1920s up until the mid 1950s were concerned not merely to catalogue folktale themes and motifs, but to establish the *Urtext* of any given oral composition. So, for example, the Finnish school's main preoccupation during this period was with gathering tale variants from all over the world with a view to tracing the archetype, place and origin of any particular story. Their purpose was to chronicle the life history of the specific tale. Many claimed that the 'same' tale could be seen to occur in various places and different times. In comparing the variants it was claimed that there remained a remarkable degree of constancy between the versions, even though certain details would change. This stability was due largely to the skill of the *raconteur*, rather than to the memory of 'primitive' story-teller. Verbatim reports were rarely given and yet the influence exerted by the community on the story-teller militated against very wide variation. The 'law' in operation was one of self-correction.[188]

This 'law', however, was not to go unchallenged. The experiments of F.C. Bartlett[189] provided verifiable evidence which refuted the 'law' of self-correction. His results showed that the degree of transformation was quite radical. Furthermore, Bartlett's findings were supported by R.H. Lowie, who specifically questioned the reliability of oral tradition for historical reconstruction.[190]

In general, this period of folklore studies was dominated by the collecting and classifying of tale types and motifs. Theories of degeneration and self-correction wre still debated, whilst attitudes associated with romantic theories of the seventeenth to nineteenth centuries were being questioned.[191] The older ideal of a folk community preserving its traditions faithfully over the centuries could no longer be substantiated. Above all it is evident that folklore was still a very young discipline, as yet formulating general principles on insufficient data.

d. *Scandinavian Scholarship*
The complexity with which the pentateuchal traditions were thought to have been transmitted has been dealt with in some detail by various Scandinavian scholars. D.H. Knight's *Rediscovering the*

Traditions of *Israel*¹⁹² provides a very clear and incisive analysis of Scandinavian scholarship, especially valuable since much of this work has not been translated. Of the eight primary characteristics of Scandinavian scholarship which D.H. Knight lists,¹⁹³ two are relevant to this discussion. The first concerns the reliability of oral traditions, and the second, the emphasis upon the supposed oral nature of the transmission and composition of the Old Testament.

In H.S. Nyberg's introduction to his study of Hosea in *Studien zum Hoseabuch*, he discussed the issues involved in the formation and transmission of the Old Testament.¹⁹⁴ His major argument was that the Hebrew text was the result of an oral transmission process which had faithfully preserved the traditions. As proof for this assumption he offered two 'facts' gained from other religious traditions. The first was the reliable way in which the *Koran* was recited, and the second was the perfect word-for-word recitation from memory of the *Yashna* by certain Parsi priests.¹⁹⁵ These ancient practices of the east were indicative of the high regard attached to oral transmission.¹⁹⁶ Hence the written text of the Old Testament was comparatively late in Israel's history, i.e. it was the creation of the post-exilic Jewish community. This was not to suggest that writing *per se* was non-existent in Israel prior to this period, but that it was reserved for administrative rather than literary purposes.¹⁹⁷ Therefore the Old Testament had been preserved and transmitted by circles of oral traditionists whose method of transmission was not mere repetition but included expansion and remoulding.¹⁹⁸ Nyberg also asserted that in the ancient Near East memory was a much more reliable means of preserving traditions than was writing.

Support for this thesis was provided by H. Birkeland,¹⁹⁹ who maintained in hs book *Zum hebräischen Traditionswesen* that a study of Islamic culture, in its treatment of the *Koran*, provided an exact analogy with the ancient Israelite preference for the spoken word. An oral tradition of reciting the *Koran* had existed alongside that of the written *Koran*, and the later transmission of the *hadith* collections was predominantly oral. The purpose of the written texts was merely to ensure the reliability of the oral transmission, although frequently the opposite happened.²⁰⁰ Birkeland argued that the Arab mentality of preferring oral to written transmission was analogous to the ancient Israelite mentality. With reference to the prophets Birkeland asserted that, although some of what they said may have been written down, oral transmission predominated.²⁰¹ In the case of the

1. Folklore Studies and Old Testament Criticism   47

pentateuchal traditions, Birkeland suggested that it may well have been the case that written sources such as J existed concomitantly with an oral source E, which gradually corrected J and resulted in the written source JE.[202]

Birkeland in his analysis of the prophetic literature maintained that the prophet's sayings had been preserved by his disciples. It was these disciples who decided which sayings were to be passed on. Throughout the period of oral transmission the material was continually reshaped and reinterpreted, with the result that we would never be able to arrive at the *ipsissima verba* of the prophet himself.[203] The form of the prophetic books as we have them, he argued, represents later literary fixations of oral tradition.

Following Nyberg and Birkeland, I. Engnell attempted to apply Nyberg's thesis of the predominance of oral tradition in the ancient Near East to the whole of the Old Testament.[204] In his article 'The Tradition-historical Method in Old Testament Research', Engnell outlines his basic methodological approach. Those aspects of the approach which have a bearing on this work are the following: 1. Exegetes who use the tradition-historical method emphasize the role played by oral tradition in the formation of the Hebrew Bible.[205] 2. Despite the variety of literary forms within the Old Testament, most of its literature, including the form of its present collection, reached a fixed state before it was written down.[206] 3. Even so, oral and written transmission should not be considered mutually exclusive. They complement each other.[207] 4. Oral transmission involves but slight transformation of the tradition. More confidence should be placed on the reliability of oral transmission of the Old Testament since it is cultic-religious literature.[208] 5. The literary historical method is therefore anachronistic and should be replaced by the tradition-historical method.[209]

On the basis of the above presuppositions, Engnell suggested that the variants within the Pentateuch were the outcome of oral transmission. Indeed he went further and claimed that a high frequency of variants was an indication that the material had been transmitted orally.[210] Referring to the epic law of iteration he argued that the literature came together and was arranged on the basis of association.[211] Rejecting the arguments underlying the documentary hypothesis as untenable on both linguistic and theological grounds,[212] Engnell maintained that contained within the Pentateuch were two originally independent collections: (1) Genesis–Numbers, which he designated as P, not because it was to be regarded as a document, but because it had many features often identified with P; (2) Deuteronomy–2 Kings, which reached its final form in a circle of traditionists designated D.[213]

This P circle of traditionists had so completely interwoven the materials of J and E at the oral level, that they were no longer distinguishable. The final written form of P was almost contemporary with D,[214] which was primarily oral. Finally, the D work was combined with the P work some time after the exile.[215]

Engnell drew five broad conclusions from this study of the Pentateuch:[216]

1. The material of the P and D traditionist circles was transmitted both in oral and written form.
2. The transcription of the material did not imply innovation, since the literature had already attained a fixed form at the oral stage.
3. Because we are dealing with sacred literature, oral transmission does not involve any more or less errors than written transmission.
4. There is a certain 'living transformation' which takes place as a result of oral transmission.
5. Although we can speak of a P and D circle of traditionists, the material has passed through many different types and kinds of traditionist circles.

To suggest that Nyberg, Birkeland and Engnell were without their critics in Scandinavia would be to present a false picture. One of the primary critics of assigning such an important role to oral transmission was G. Widengren. He rejected the assumption that analogies could be drawn from other Near Eastern religions to substantiate arguments for the primacy of oral transmission. Instead he asserted that it was impossible to ascertain whether or not oral as opposed to written means of transmission had been operative in ancient Israel. Indeed it was incorrect to contrast these two means.[217] Both Arabic[218] and Mesopotamian[219] cultures testified to a tendency within Near Eastern cultures to commit oral traditions to writing at quite an early stage. Furthermore, since there was no mention in the Old Testament of circles of traditionists who preserved material through oral transmission, less importance should be attributed to this means of transmission.[220]

1. *Folklore Studies and Old Testament Criticism*

It would seem that G. Widengren refused the possibility of establishing the pre-literary form of a text, and certainly denied that the period of oral transmission was a long one. Many of Widengren's assertions had yet to be substantiated by folklore studies. More recently, however, certain studies on oral composition and transmission of narrative have been carried out which would seem to vindicate his stance. These will be discussed in Chapter 2.

Although E. Nielson's conclusions on oral composition and transmission were but a restatement of Nyberg, Birkeland and Engnell, he has provided a helpful list of criteria by which to distinguish oral from written transmission of tradition.

Where traditions occur only once, Nielson argued that the following criteria should be used to identify the oral original behind the written text:[221]

1. The traditions have a monotonous style, and contain recurrent expressions.
2. They are composed in a fluent and paratactic style.
3. There is anacoluthia.
4. The traditions conform to Olrik's Epic Laws.

If the tradition occurred more than once, then Nielson argued that the kind of variation between the two would determine whether or not it was a graphic or phonetic variation.[222]

What this list clearly shows is that the criteria for establishing orality had hardly shifted from Gunkel's day.

7. *Has Progress Been Made in the Understanding of Oral Composition and Transmission?*

The debate concerning oral as opposed to written tradition has not always distinguished between issues of composition and those of transmission. Too often tradition-historical approaches have relied upon the findings of Gunkel and not questioned the validity of the criteria used to distinguish originally oral from written compositions. This was understandable, since among folklorists Olrik's criteria long remained unchallenged.[223] It seemed reasonable to assume that the forms of originally oral composition units could therefore be established, and since these units were regarded as the products of primitive societies, a general *Sitz im Leben*, i.e. that of the premonarchic period, could be established. Moreover even where Old

Testament scholars (e.g. Westermann, von Rad, Noth) were dependent on Jolles for their understanding of the patriarchal narratives, the only resultant change was in relocating these stories within the sociological setting of the family. The analysis of their form, however, was dependent on Gunkel's and therefore Olrik's laws. How far these 'laws' can now be accepted will be discussed in Chapter 2 along with some preliminary suggestions regarding the creation of oral composition and the possibility of distinguishing these from written texts.

Issues surrounding oral transmission rather than composition are even more complicated. A professional guild of story-tellers, tribal narrators or trained traditionists have all been suggested as transmitters of tradition. There has been no agreement, however, as to the extent of fixity and/or change which may have taken place in the transmission of the narratives over an extended period of time. Nor has there been unanimity as to whether or not they contain data which is historically reliable. For Engnell, and to some extent for Noth, oral transmission implied a 'living transformation' of the material. With Noth, however, one is left with the impression that although he believes that the different parts of the Pentateuch have coalesced gradually over an extended period of time and the original core has been supplemented by other narratives, it is still possible to uncover the original nucleus of the individual themes. Therefore for Noth the process presumes faithful transmission over an extended period of time.

Before a judgment can be made as to the truth or otherwise of his position, further knowledge of the mechanisms of oral narrative composition and transmission is needed. The next chapter will therefore turn to the more recent research undertaken by folklorists to see what light they throw on the question.

Chapter 2

FOLK NARRATIVE:
ITS COMPOSITION AND TRANSMISSION

1. *Oral Narrative Composition*

Our understanding of the technique of oral narrative composition has in the past two decades undergone a radical revision in the light of the fieldwork of M. Parry and A.B. Lord. Their interest was initially with the Homeric literature, and therefore the impact which their work has had on biblical studies has quite naturally been in the area of poetic rather than prose narrative studies.[1] More recently, however, Lord has turned his attention to the study of prose narratives, where his conclusions have clear ramifications for the study of oral narratives in general.

Starting with the Homeric literature Parry argued that the high frequency of formulaic epithets, phrases and repeated word groups found in the *Odyssey* and *Iliad* were indications of oral composition.[2] The epic poet, Parry suggested, would have had at his disposal certain formulae which he would have combined in various ways. These formulae would have acted like building blocks, and by combining them the poet could use traditional material, while still creating his own composition. It was precisely these formulae which would have allowed the poet the means by which to recite such lengthy poems as the *Iliad* and the *Odyssey* without having to rely solely upon memory.

Having arrived at these theoretical conclusions, Parry, assisted by Lord, attempted to substantiate them by undertaking a study of the oral poetry techniques of Yugoslavian bards. Parry died in 1935 but his work was continued by Lord, and published in the *Singer of Tales*.[3] This concluded that the manner in which the bard composed his epic song was identical to that postulated by Parry for the poets of the *Iliad* and *Odyssey*. Like the epic poet, the bard did not memorize his epic song. Instead, he used certain formulae, stores in his memory to be used at various moments in his recitation.[4] These formulae, far from creating a rigidity of composition, allowed the bard to alter the song by manipulating the formulae for each performance and/or substituting different words in the formulae. But Lord argued that the formulae themselves were not as important as their underlying patterns and the singer's ability to create different phrases according to the pattern.[5] The pattern was not confined to a single line but could be represented in certain line sequences[6] which could result in large groups of lines being part of a pattern.[7]

In addition to these formulaic phrases the bard also had certain set themes (i.e. groups of ideas)[8] which could be used in structuring a poem, as well as set plots,[9] all of which could be combined in different ways. The result of this technique was that the bard would actually compose during a performance. Consequently there could be no concept of a fixed text,[10] for each performance of the song was a new creation. Therefore, no longer could one speak of the original song, and hence if there is no original there can be no variants:

> The truth of the matter is that our concept of 'the original' of 'the song' simply makes no sense in oral tradition... It follows then, that we cannot correctly speak of a variant since there is no original to be varied.[11]

Although a bard may sing the same song twice it is never word-for-word repetition. Each performance is unique and will involve the utilization of different formulaic phrases.

Thus, it was argued that, at least for poetry, formulaic phrases were an indication of oral composition. They both allowed for composition during performance and enabled the poet to compose very long poems without having to rely on memory. Furthermore, Lord had demonstrated that the concept of an original text in oral composition could no longer be upheld.

These findings represented a significant shift in the understanding of how oral composition took place. Changes in the poetic narrative which according to the previous approach had been attributed to corruption were now seen to be an integral part of the very techniques of oral composition. Whereas one can identify an originally oral text by its high frequency of formulaic phrases, it is impossible to determine compositional variants, much less transmission variants.

Such conclusions are themselves open to question, however. Just how far does density of formulaic style indicate oral composition? Presumably all that would be required to answer this question in the negative would be enough evidence to show that oral poets could compose without recourse to the frequent use of formulae. Lord himself admitted the possibility that a talented bard might not need to use such formulae.[12] As far as he was concerned, however, this was the exception rather than the rule. L.D. Benson's[13] and J. Opland's[14] results question the very basis of Lord's work. They have shown that the high frequency of formulaic phrases is no sure guide to orality, since they can be found in texts which were known to have been originally written. A yet more fundamental question remains unanswered by Lord, namely, what constitutes a formula and what percentage of formulas is needed before a composition can be considered oral? Unless these are defined, judgments as to their presence or absence, frequency or otherwise are impossible.

If Lord in his appeal to the 'formulaic' in oral composition can be accused of failing to define his terms, in other aspects of his work his definitions seem far too rigid. So when it comes to insisting that all oral poetry is composition in performance, he is as dogmatic as those who had primarily defined oral poetry as the memorization of a fixed text. The evidence, however, would suggest a more complex reality. R. Finnegan, for example, has shown that there are instances where oral poets will compose a poem and then not perform it until they have memorized it.[15] Between these two extremes exist any number of permutations ranging from improvisation to memorization of oral composition.[16] Sweeping generalizations about the nature of oral composition, as proposed by Lord in *The Singer of Tales*, cannot therefore be substantiated. What obtained in the case of the Yugoslavian bards cannot be said to be true of all forms of oral composition:

> The relationships between composition, memorization and performance in oral poetry is more open than the definite sounding term 'oral composition' seems to imply. The 'oral formulaic' style of composition . . . is not a sufficient indication for concluding that a given work is 'oral', nor a necessary condition for the creation of 'oral poetry'.[17]

Some of the conclusions reached by Lord concerning the composition of oral poetry were subsequently applied by him to oral prose, in an introductory article to a collection of Angolan tales.[18] Here Lord suggested that the story-teller, like the poet, will avail himself of set patterns and incidents and that the presence of such repeated patterns and incidents is a sure indication of oral composition.[19] Lord's comments, however, are not based on his own field study but are rather the generalized conclusions taken from one field study and applied to all oral compositions. What was true for the composition of epic poetry was also true for prose:

> This is the kind of panorama that is characteristic of story material in the oral tradition be it in prose or verse, be it 'primitive' or 'advanced'... the patterned mingling of themes... is the same as those seen in oral epic among the Southern Slavs and in such cultural masterpieces as the *Iliad* and the *Odyssey*.[20]

In a more recent study, however, Lord has been more reluctant to apply rigid formulaic analysis as proof of oral composition, and states that our knowledge in the area is still incomplete.[21] Furthermore, he admits that a clear distinction between oral and written traditional style is not always possible, given that a poet may adopt an oral formulaic technique and apply it to a written text.[22] Lord has, however, remained adamant regarding the issue of memorization, although now he has confined his remarks to the techniques of oral composition employed by the Slavic Balkan bards. Memory plays a role in the process but only with regard to certain fixed formulae, and even then the memorization is unconscious:

> Memorization requires a fixed text and is impossible in the oral traditional narrative poetries with which I am acquainted, because in the tradition's natural state there are no fixed texts to memorize. The singers of the South Slavs are creators and not rhapsodes as is sometimes erroneously averred by those who do not comprehend their art.[23]

Lord suggests that the role memory plays will fluctuate given different genres, and that this must be taken into consideration when speaking about relative degrees of fixity.[24] Nevertheless, Lord was prepared in an earlier article to state that 'in narrative, particularly longer narrative, an oral fixed text is impossible'.[25] Lord speaks of a 'textual fluidity' which does not accommodate the notion of 'word for word' retelling of a set, established text. For Lord, transmission is in fact composition.[26] These remarks of Lord's however, are on the purely hypothetical level. As R. Finnegan has shown there are

2. Folk Narrative: Its Composition and Transmission

enough case studies available to indicate that oral narration can include everything from a new creation to memorized reproduction.[27]

It would seem from this brief survey that even on Lord's own admission, the oral-formulaic theory of oral composition is not as monolithic as might otherwise have been assumed. Scholars working within Homeric studies have cast similar doubts upon many of Lord's conclusions.[28]

In our discussion of Gunkel's criteria for establishing the original oral composition of a text, that of repetition was mentioned.[29] In her comprehensive study on oral poetry, R. Finnegan totally rejects the idea of using repetition as a touchstone for distinguishing 'oral' from 'written' composition style:

> The concept of repetition is itself too wide. When one considers its many manifestations it turns out often to mean little more than recurrent patterns. If one tries to make it more precise (as in the repetition of incidents only,[30] or particular types of stylistic repetition) the theory loses its apparent universality and thus its appeal. The frequent recurrence of 'formulae'—or their appearance in measurable number—used to be taken as a sufficient condition for calling a composition 'oral', but 'formulaic' literary style is equally possible in written literature.[31]

To delineate between oral and written composition style on the basis of 'oral formulaic' theories of repetition is inadequate. The situation is much more complex. Whereas the theory may hold true for certain kinds of composition in some societies, no universal statements can or should be made. In fact the complexities involved in distinguishing oral from written style are such as to suggest the impossibility of reaching any conclusion which would determine the original oral or written form of a particular Old Testament passage. This is not to imply that there are no differences between oral and written versions of narratives. However, in situations where the same stylistic features occur in both written and oral compositions, these cannot be used as criteria for differentiating an originally oral version from the written version.[32]

What then of the frequent use by folklorists (at least until recently) of Olrik's criteria? In Chapter 1 it was pointed out that the use of Olrik's 'Epic Laws' has also persisted among biblical scholars, their most recent utilization being found in the work of J. Van Seters' *Abraham in History and Tradition*.[33] The extent to which these 'Epic Laws' can be relied upon as an indication of oral rather than written composition is far from certain, as recent folklore studies have shown.

In his article of 1909,[34] Olrik attempted to establish universally held laws of oral composition. These were thirteen in number and they could be seen to be reflected in all oral genres. They consisted of:

1. A clear opening and closing.
2. Repetition.
3. Never more than three or four characters.
4. Never more than two to a scene.
5. A use of character contrast.
6. The presence of twins or two of a kind.
7. The initial character is always balanced by the last character.
8. The narrative only has a single strand.
9. Marked patterning.
10. Tableau scenes are used climactically.
11. The narrative conforms to its own internal logic.
12. A unity of plot.
13. The narrative always concentrates on a leading character.

If any given narrative adhered to these laws, then it could be considered to have been originally oral.

Olrik's conclusions, although based on his long experience as a folklorist, were nevertheless largely theoretical rather than empirical. Furthermore, the basis of his criteria has since been proved to be untenable, not least because the material upon which Olrik established his epic laws had itself been edited in the process of transcription.[35] The material upon which Olrik based his conclusions, therefore, had undergone radical changes in both content and form. For example, many of the stories had been reduced in length to an 'essential' core.[36] Therefore, methodologically, Olrik's laws of folk narrative composition were based on faulty texts. These were not examples of verbatim transcription. This factor alone should convince us of the validity of D. Tedlock's warning against attempting to:

> develop an effective oral poetics if we begin with structural analysis of conventional written texts, whether those texts were created by ancient scribes or modern field workers.[37]

That Olrik's laws have recently been seen to apply to both oral and written texts can be regarded as acknowledgment of these criticisms

2. Folk Narrative: Its Composition and Transmission

and a correction of Olrik's original work. In an attempt to discover just how different oral texts are from written ones dealing with the same subject matter, L. Danielson applied eight of Olrik's thirteen 'Epic Laws' to some 143 texts. The results were clearly unexpected. Of the eight laws seven were seen to operate in terms of content, structure and style in the same way for oral as for written texts. So high was the correlation that the seven functioned in both kinds of narrative at 'roughly the same intensity'.[38]

Recently the work of J. Pentikäinen in collecting the oral repertoire of one traditionist, Marina Takalo, has also brought Olrik's laws into question. What has emerged is that Olrik's laws do not apply to all genre categories.[39] On the basis of his study Pentikäinen has concluded that Olrik's laws pertain to only one genre, that of the folktale.[40] Whereas Pentikäinen considers the laws useful in relation to the folktale, he warns against using Olrik's hypothetical rules as proven 'laws':

> As far as oral communication is concerned Olrik's 'laws' should be studied as hypotheses which nevertheless should be tested, taking into account both the differences between genres and the entire holistic communication process both as an individual and as a social phenomenon.[41]

The most striking aspect of these criticisms of Olrik's work is that no one previously thought to test his conclusions. What is clearly emerging now is that his 'Epic Laws' cannot be used as universal truths of oral narrative composition. They can no longer be accepted as super-organic laws to which the forms of oral genres adhere. The implication for biblical studies is clear, for it should consequently affect our acceptance of many of Gunkel's conclusions (themselves similar to those of Olrik) about the nature and form of oral composition.

The most recent study to deal with issues relating to the nature of oral narrative composition and transmission in the patriarchal narratives is Van Seters' *Abraham in History and Tradition*. This is a radical re-evaluation of the sources of the Abraham tradition in the Pentateuch, together with their dating. This new approach arises out of his unease with present literary and historical-critical method. He has argued that since there are not absolute reasons for dating the Genesis material in the second millennium BCE of a hypothetical patriarchal age, an alternative can and should be suggested.

First, he acknowledges the need to establish the unity or diversity of the sources involved in the Abraham tradition. Van Seters then puts forward his reasons (i.e. doublets in plot and theme, and contradictions between stories[42]) for believing that the Abraham tradition must have been composed from a plurality of sources. Recognizing that disunity can also occur within stories, he suggests that it is a legitimate task to attempt to determine which part of the story is primary and which secondary. Where a story is obviously the result of a combination of earlier versions, the story itself must be considered a new literary work. Van Seters criticizes reconstructions based on hypothetical sources as too subjective and rejects such a method.

The relationship between the sources is a complex issue. The orthodox position has always been to argue their independence of each other. Any similarity has always been accounted for by appealing to a common core tradition (e.g. Noth's *Grundlage*). Van Seters rejects this theory since, first, it is impossible to substantiate if this common core is thought of as having been oral. He points out that the concept of a fixed oral prose tradition is a fictitious one which has been disproved by folklorists. Second, the notion of faithful transmission has also been disproved. Finally, Van Seters argues that in a literate society there is a tendency to commit to writing those traditions which are beneficial to the state.[43]

Van Seters rejects the possibility of identifying the particular genre(s) of the Abraham stories, stating that most folklorists are agreed that the singular difference between the genres of myth, legend, historical narrative and folktales, is one of belief, which of itself is no indication of how historically reliable the narrative is. Gunkel's use of the term legend (*Sage*) was meant to indicate not only certain specific characteristics of the form but also that it had derived from a situation of oral story-telling. But, as Van Seters points out, this association 'says nothing about the period of origin or degree to which the present literary form derives from oral tradition'.[44] However, although the first part of the statement is valid and undermines Gunkel's assumptions about a pre-literate period of story-telling, the second is not so convincing since the legend by definition implies an oral composition genre.

If Van Seters wishes to imply that, given a piece of writing, underlying oral sources are almost impossible to detect, whether the genre be myth, legend (*Sage*) or folktale, then I can concur. But this does not seem to be his point, since he appeals to Olrik's laws as indicators of the 'sources of a narrator and his mode of composition'.[45]

I have already maintained that recourse cannot be made to these 'epic laws' to differentiate between oral and written composition. Van Seters himself on occasion mentions that modern folklorists have raised objections to the use of these laws. Furthermore, he admits that most of the narratives in Genesis fit Olrik's laws very poorly. Nonetheless, he uses them himself. Like Olrik before him, however, he never indicates just how many laws a narrative must fulfil in order to be classified as oral. Are some more important than others? If so, which are the most crucial?

There is some confusion surrounding Olrik's second law of folk (oral) narrative composition, i.e. that of repetition (*das Gesetz der Wiederholung*), and since Van Seters uses this law to substantiate the oral nature of Gen. 12.10-20, a more detailed discussion is necessary at this point.

Referring to the fact that written literature has many ways of producing emphasis, Olrik states that oral narrative has only one, and that is repetition. It both builds up tension and expands the body of the narrative.[46] Here Olrik makes a distinction between what he calls 'intensifying repetition' and 'simple repetition', but unfortunately he does not elaborate on what it is that constitutes the difference between the two.

Generally speaking, repetition is an ill-defined phenomenon. Thus R. Kellog, in an attempt to give a brief and highly generalized description of what constitutes oral narrative, refers to repetition as an aspect of its rhythmic quality. The rhythm may in some instances consist in part of rhythmic gestures, dances or chanting of the performer. It may also be derived from structural rhythms such as stanzas, refrains and repeated motifs or temporal repetitions of all sorts.[47] Lord attempted to distinguish between two kinds of repetition: (a) where an incident is repeated within the same plot, and (b) where an incident is retold within the narrative. For Lord, both of these were sub-categories of the kind of repetition of theme which occurs between stories (for example the wife/sister theme in Gen. 12.10-20; 20; 26.1-6).[48] Olrik, however, in enumerating his laws did so in terms of their applicability to each individual story and not groups or cycles of stories. Thus, the term 'repetition' can be used in two distinct ways. The first refers to repetition *within a work* and is an oral composition, whereas repetition of incidents *from work to work* constitutes the oral tradition. Similarly, a distinction in the verbal features of oral literature may be made, whereby 'convention' is the term used to signify a verbal construct that recurs from work to work, and 'formula' is used to signify a verbal construct that is repeated within a work.

Tracing the repetition of incidents from work to work has been a particular mark of the historico-geographic school of folktale research. this is not to suggest that the occurrence of a particular incident in different tales is any measure of their oral character. Folklorists freely admit that evidence of such recurrence is not confined to oral stories but is also found in written works of literature.

It has been argued that repetition, as reflected in formulae and repeated incidents within a story, however, is an indication of an orally composed narrative. Thus after an analysis of two stories, *The Vampire*[49] and *Pretty Maid Ibronka*,[50] B. Gray concluded that duplication of incident is the chief principle of oral composition, whereas description of incident is the chief principle of written composition. Gray maintained this even though he admitted that there are occasions when such descriptions can also be found within orally composed narrative. In the light of this, he warns against using even this particular phenomenon as the infallible touchstone for detecting orally composed narratives:

> It is possible though not common for something to be originated and even transmitted orally without exhibiting repetition.[51]

Therefore in any recourse to Olrik's law of repetition it must be borne in mind that Olrik was referring to repetition (both verbal and incidental) *within a story*, and that although such repetition is normally manifested in oral composition it is not inevitably so. It is not possible, therefore, to regard Olrik's second law as a universal truth. Just how unreliable this law is as a test of orality is indicated by Gray, who observed that this criterion had still to be tested, and that by 1971, 'no one in anthropology, folklore or literature has undertaken any systematic analysis of repetition in folk and primitive literature'.[52] To my knowledge the only subsequent study of oral composition which has attempted a systematic application of Olrik's laws to both written and oral texts of the same story is that of L. Danielson, which I have already mentioned.

2. Folk Narrative: Its Composition and Transmission   61

In addition to discussing how one can determine whether or not a written text has been composed from oral sources, Van Seters deals with issues of transmission and compositional variants. He rejects the possibility that the doublets in Genesis are the result of a transmission process (whether written or oral). He argues that the versions are too distinct to have arisen out of scribal error, and oral transmission variants would only occur if there were a fixed body of oral tradition—a phenomenon which Van Seters considers most improbable.

Besides transmission variants there are also oral and written compositional variants which Van Seters maintains are distinguishable from one another. He offers the following criteria for establishing literary compositional variants:

1. The simplest form and structure of an account is most likely to be the earliest one.
2. Whereas the second version of an account tends to summarize, it may also add new material and thereby produce a longer story.
3. Sometimes in a later version there are 'blind motifs' which assume knowledge of an earlier version of the same story.
4. Verbal similarity is an indication of literary dependence, unless such similarities are popular sayings and/or common expressions.[53]

On the other hand, oral composition variants (by which Van Seters means any theme or plot which is used in more than one tale by either the same or a different story-teller) are usually: (1) found in the same genre, differing in non-typical detail. The same theme may migrate to different genres, but a combination of genres is a literary rather than an oral phenomenon; (2) not summarized. The tradent more often only manages one form and therefore any new material is added in the same genre; (3) lacking in the knowledge of all aspects of a story, and therefore the 'blind motif' as such does not exist in oral variants. If an important aspect has been lost from lapse of memory the story-teller will have to supply something new.[54]

Having made these distinctions Van Seters proceeds to analyze the doublets found in the Abraham tradition. These, he suggests, will inform us as to whether or not the tradition developed from the literary dependence of one source on the other, or from a common use of oral tradition. Such an analysis will reveal the essential characteristics of each source, thus allowing Van Seters to assign the remaining parts of the tradition to their respective sources.

Van Seters' remarks concerning written composition variants are orthodox in conception, although caution is called for if his first rule, that of the 'simplest' form being the earliest, is to be used.[55] His comments concerning oral composition variants, however, are not so universally accepted and it would have been helpful had Van Seters given some indication as to the basis of these assertions. The only reference he gives is to A.B. Lord's *The Singer of Tales*. If this study is the basis of his generalizations then genre classification becomes very important. For what may be true for a Yugoslavian bard's oral song composition technique is certainly not necessarily true of ancient Israelite story-telling technique.[56]

Furthermore, Van Seters makes the assertion that oral composition variants do not summarize.[57] This simplistic position does not warrant close scrutiny. If Van Seters is dependent on Lord's *The Singer of Tales*, then his whole discussion of oral composition variants is invalid. If there is no concept of an original oral composition then there can be no variant. Van Seters offers no other evidence for his evaluation. He defines a variant as similar material occurring in different works either by the same or different authors. Of course, in order to speak meaningfully of a variant it has to be a variant of an original or *Ur-form*. In order to reconstruct this original the various texts have to be rearranged in order to correspond to what the *Urtext* is thought to have looked like. Given Van Seters' criteria, the more original form of a text whose theme or plot has variants will be the simplest. This does not of itself tell us whether the *Urtext* was originally oral or written. This is not Van Seters' primary concern. His purpose is clear; it is to trace the historical development of the Abraham tradition. In order to undertake such an enterprise he assumes the existence of the *Urform* of the text. For Van Seters this is a separate source on which all the others are based. It is the variants found in the treatment of the wife/sister stories in Genesis 12, 20 and 26 which provide the fulcrum of his argument, for these form the basis of his source divisions.

Van Seters argues that Genesis 12 forms the basis of ch. 20 and ch. 26. It is the earliest of the three stories. Genesis 12 may therefore be regarded as the *Urtext*. Van Seters may well be right that chs. 20 and 26 are dependent on ch. 12. What is not so convincing, however, is that ch. 12 is the written version of an oral folktale. In an attempt to

2. Folk Narrative: Its Composition and Transmission

establish its orality Van Seters uses two sets of criteria. The first is Olrik's epic laws, which we have already indicated cannot be used to distinguish between oral and written texts. The second criterion is that of folktales which share similar themes. He detects their structure in Genesis 12. Just how legitimate it is to compare twentieth-century folktales with biblical material, however, is questionable.[58] On the basis of 'blind motifs' Van Seters argues that ch. 20 presumes ch. 12 and that Gen. 26.1-11 is a conflation of the two. Extending this argument he includes the narratives of the covenant between Abimelech and Abraham in Gen. 21.22-34 and 26.12-33, both of which he maintains belong to the Yahwist source. It is unnecessary here to rehearse Van Seters' intricate argument. My purpose is simply to query the possibility of identifying an oral folktale behind a written text.

For Van Seters there is no need to postulate separate redactors, 'because the process was supplementary and the later authors were the redactors of the earlier material as well'.[59] In this he may well be right, but what has not been proved is that a source consisting of oral and folktale-like material ever existed, let alone in the fragmentary form suggested by Van Seters.

On issues of dating Van Seters has suggested that the Yahwistic source should be placed in the exile and that the priestly source is post-exilic. The Yahwistic source is dependent on an earlier written pre-Yahwistic one, the date of which he does not stipulate. For Van Seters there is no subsequent Elohist source.

In considering oral tradition, Van Seters has quite properly undermined the simplistic equation which identifies orality with antiquity. He has not, however, resolved the problems inherent in any attempt to identify the originally oral form of the written biblical text. Whereas in his discussion of Genesis 12 he maintains that it is earlier than ch. 20 or ch. 26 since the latter are dependent upon it, he nevertheless appeals to Olrik's laws to establish ch. 12 as having originally been an oral composition.

In maintaining the essentially oral character of ch. 12 and 16.1-10, Van Seters has provided an explanation for their common form and structure which is not found in any other Abraham material. He attributes this to the pre-Yahwistic stage one source.[60] Against this, however, it should be pointed out that the resemblance which these sections have to oral folktale material is debatable, and, as we have seen, distinctions between oral and written material based on Olrik's epic laws are unreliable. A denial of the basic orality of the source, however, would not seriously undermine Van Seters' reconstruction of the Abraham tradition.[61] He would, nonetheless, need to provide an alternative explanation which would account for the similarities found in the material of his pre-Yahwistic stage one source.

Another major problem with accepting this material as a separate source, apart form its brevity, is to explain why the culture would have preserved these stories and thought them sufficiently important to develop in either oral or written form. It is significant that Van Seters does not discuss the matter of transmission. He could have avoided the problems of establishing an oral pre-text if he had chosen to amalgamate stages one and two of his pre-Yahwistic source, and accepted the combination as a written source, which underwent considerable expansion during the exilic period. Be that as it may, unless Van Seters can offer other criteria by which to establish oral from written material, it is difficult to accept his hypothetical source division.

So far it has been argued that the usual indicators of oral composition are not as foolproof as had once been thought. Does this mean, then, that there is no specific oral style? For Gunkel, oral style was an unconscious and spontaneous poetic expression of the primitive mind. Today similar notions of the primitive mentality are reflected in the works of W.J. Ong[62] and J. Goody.[63] While rejecting the term 'primitive', nonetheless both maintain that there is a cognitive consequence of literacy. So, for example, literacy allows for abstract and logical thinking, whereas non-literates can only think concretely. Literacy is therefore considered to be essential for analytical processes. However, as D. Tannen has reminded us, there have been enough studies carried out to indicate that literacy does not lead to significant cognitive differences. What these studies have shown is that the same basic mental functions occur in adults of any culture, literate or non-literate.[64] The form and content of Gunkel's legend designation cannot be identified as the product of primitive man or necessarily non-literate man. R. Finnegan has warned against adopting too simplistic a view of 'unconscious' composition and dismisses the idea of the '"typical" oral artist as "primaeval" and "natural" man, who acts unconsciously and through "nature" rather than art'.[65]

In discussing the possibility of more formal indications of oral composition, such as repetition and formulaic language, I have suggested that whereas these are aspects of oral compositions, they are inadequate criteria upon which to base distinctions between oral and written compositions.

For Finnegan the most important aspect of an 'oral' style is the performance. It is this element which most clearly distinguishes oral from written compositions. We should look to the performance 'as well as the bare text' for specific distinguishing characteristics.[66] More precise criteria for determining a specific oral style are not possible. But as Finnegan reminds us:

> If the line between oral and written cannot be drawn with any precision, why should there be two distinct styles differentiated by a single crucial factor?[67]

It is this aspect of performance which needs to be studied for a more complete understanding of orality. In so far as folklore is 'verbal art' which is communicated by tradition bearers, then the way it is transmitted and what happens in the process of transmission are important elements.

2. Oral Narrative Transmission

In Chapter 1 it was argued that the relative fixity of OT material at the oral stage was an issue on which there was little agreement amongst biblical scholars. A whole range of opinion could be found, from total rejection of ever being able to establish what was once the original oral form of a tradition, to Gunkel's belief that such forms were distinguishable, and had been reliably transmitted by a 'professional class of story-tellers'. Nyberg, Birkeland, Engnell and Nielson maintained that whereas the original form cannot be uncovered, these traditions originated at the oral stage and were only slightly transformed by the tradition circles which transmitted them—a process which in some cases lasted hundreds of years.

But just exactly how much do we know of how individual stories, let alone whole tradition cycles (or in Gunkel's case legend cycles) were transmitted? Is there such a thing as a fixed oral tradition which is passed on faithfully from one generation to the next? What are the methods which are employed in oral transmission? How far can we distinguish oral transmission variants from literary transmission variants, once given a written text? These issues were discussed briefly by Van Seters, who suggested that in the category of literary transmission variants should be included 'scribal errors, deviations, additions which will vary according to the canonicity of the text and the care and competence of the copyists'.[68] As regards oral transmission variants, these, Van Seters argued, would occur whenever an oral tradition was considered fixed, and passed on by means of memorization.[69] He did not, however, accept that the Old Testament material fell into this category. K. Koch has claimed that variants may occur in oral transmission when words are replaced by others which sound alike or when 'an obsolete word is changed'.[70] However, it is debatable just how far both these possibilities necessarily indicate oral transmission variants. In the case of the former, it is possible that errors of this sort could be the result of a scribe transcribing an already written text which was being dictated to him. One may call this an oral transmission variant, but it tells us nothing about the tradition itself. The tradition might or might not be oral. In the case of Koch's second suggestion, once given a written text it is impossible to establish what has or has not been changed at the oral stage. These two types of variant could be considered written transmission variants.

As has been noted in Chapter 1, certain Scandinavian scholars have concluded that whereas traditions were reshaped as they were being transmitted, nonetheless overall stability and reliability were maintained. On the one hand those responsible for transmitting the traditions were not merely involved in a passive memorization of the tradition; on the other they ensured its continued life by adding to it new material and subtracting from it material which was no longer relevant. This position inevitably leads us to ask: How far is memorization a reliable means of transmitting traditions? How accurate is the memory?

First, we must consider the idea of a fixed oral tradition which is handed down verbatim.

The work of J. Pentikäinen[71] has produced some interesting results in this field of study. Very rarely have folklorists been interested in the tradition bearer. In this case the name of the tradition bearer was Marina Takalo, an illiterate, who was born in Russia in 1890 and died in 1970. The study of her oral repertoire of stories was conducted by Pentikäinen over a period of thirty years. The approach to oral transmission typified by the Finnish geographico-historical method was to consider diffusion as a straightforward mechanical process, irrespective of the people responsible for that transmission. This approach was criticized by von Sydow, who stated that:

2. Folk Narrative: Its Composition and Transmission

> every tradition has its custodians, tradition being bound up with various social circles. Thus if we are to understand how a tradition is disseminated we must first examine the milieu from which it originates.[72]

Against the Finnish school, von Sydow argued that traditions did not simply spread of their own accord, but were transmitted by bearers of tradition, each of whom had distinctive methods of communication. It was not enough only to know what was transmitted; one had also to understand who was responsible for its transmission.

For Olrik this was immaterial, since all oral genres were subject to laws which themselves controlled the individual story-teller. The cognitive processes of the tradition bearer did not matter, since the tradition itself was governed by these laws.

Lord's conception of a free composition in performance meant that composition became identified with transmission. Each singer, therefore, used traditional material but never in an identical way. The skill of the epic bard was all-important, as it was in the case of Dégh's story-tellers.[73] Like the Yugoslavian bard who combined and manipulated given formulae, Dégh's story-tellers had stock themes and motifs which they would use to reshape traditional tales.

Since the 1960s there has been a considerable shift in the way folklorists believe oral transmission operates:

> One mistake made by folklorists in the past has been to regard storytelling as a stereotyped process that could not be changed in its details and that always followed a fixed pattern. Yet studies have shown that each story-telling situation is unique by nature; it is an event that occurs only once in the temporal, spatial and social circumstances.[74]

In his study of M. Takalo, Pentikäinen points out time and again just how much an oral tradition is transformed in the transmission process.[75] Not only were the circumstances important in transforming Takalo's repertoire but her own personality contributed as well to the process:

> Marina Takalo's repertoire of folklore did not seem to be any stable unchangeable whole, rather it appeared to change in accordance with the development of the individual personality and the epochs of her life history.[76]

The degree to which M. Takalo influenced the transmission process was significant even though the extent of change was dependent on the genre of the material. Therefore, it would seem that the importance of distinguishing between different genres should not be underestimated. (The issue of genre analysis will be discussed in Chapter 3.) The extent to which any item of tradition is already accepted also will exert a corresponding influence on the way it is transmitted.[77]

What is also significant in M. Takalo's repertoire is what J. Pentikäinen refers to as 'memorized knowledge'. Pentikäinen distinguishes this from tradition, which with Lord he defines as 'culture (elements) handed down from one generation to another'. For him 'memorized knowledge' involves different cognitive mechanisms and should not be equated with tradition. Unlike tradition, 'memorized knowledge' is prone to different sorts of transformation, themselves related to loss of memory and contamination.[78]

Finnegan is unable to produce any studies which would substantiate the claim that word-for-word reproduction over long periods of time is typical of oral transmission. Whereas examples of word-perfect memorization can be quoted where a written text is available,[79] where no such texts exist:

> The emphasis now and for some time in the past has been on 'variants', the differing verbal forms in which what is in some sense 'the same' basic piece of plot is expressed.[80]

The theory that memory is untrustworthy and that this accounts for variants has long had its adherents in both folklore and biblical studies. So it is maintained that where tradition offers us very little information about a particular character and/or event here we have the remnants of a very ancient folk tradition. It is along these lines that, for example, M. Noth argues for the priority of Isaac over Abraham:

> Now the fact that Isaac recedes into the background in contrast to Abraham, the figure that manifestly evolved later, speaks for Isaac's priority. In comparison to Isaac, therefore, Abraham is to be regarded as the more 'modern' figure who, at the expense of Isaac, obtained more and more space in the tradition.[81]

Folklore studies, as represented by the work of J.R. Moore at the turn of the century, was very much influenced by theories of degeneration in transmission. Moore's position has much in common with Van Seters and Koch with regard to oral transmission:

2. Folk Narrative: Its Composition and Transmission

There are certain factors at work in the mind of the singer to destroy or to sustain his memory of the ballads. In the first place there is a natural tendency to obliviscence, by which things of a former year tend to make way for things of the present moment. Again, changes take place in the meaning or pronunciation of words, thereby obscuring the singer's memory. Similarly, words which lack associative significance are likely to drop out and be replaced by something else, especially in the case of proper names and obsolete words.[82]

The degree of memorization as it relates to composition has been discussed with reference to Lord's oral formulaic theories. As regards a supposed degeneration process, it is interesting to note that folklorists no longer consider oral variants to be a product of faulty memorization but are more and more stressing the aspect of 're-creation' in oral transmission.[83] Memorization as a technique, however, can still result in exact reproduction:

> In any tradition there will be some individuals who are primarily uncreative in verbal terms and, so far as they take part in the transmission of actual texts, tend to pass on forms in much the shape they received them though perhaps in an imperfect form due to imperfect remembering.[84]

Nonetheless, in the majority of cases, where traditions are assumed to have been passed on through many centuries:

> The whole linguistic complexion of the piece may be so modified with the development of the language in which it is composed, that the original author would not recognize his work if he heard it recited. Taken collectively these processes of oral tradition amount to a second act of composition.[85]

This recreation often utilizes stock themes, phrases and plots which the tradition transmitter will rely on when telling a story.

We must also ask whether or not the reliability of transmission is directly related to its particular standing within the community. In other words, if a tradition is contained within a religious and liturgical context, does this of itself guarantee faithful transmission?[86]

With reference to the *Rgveda* and the claims of various Indian scholars that its faithful transmission has been due to memorization, R. Finnegan expresses certain doubts. These doubts have been raised equally by Old Testament scholars as to the exact oral transmission of the traditions contained within the received text. Since we have no extant, pre-exilic version of many of these traditions, we have no 'control' text with which to monitor the kinds of change which may have occurred. Nevertheless:

> Where there are strong religious sanctions on continuity there is less likelihood of variation (though it is not impossible) and diffusion is often relatively straightforward.[87]

The operative phrase here is 'strong religious sanctions', for we have no way of measuring how the ancient Israelite would have regarded his religious traditions. Bearing this in mind, the overwhelming weight of evidence indicates that the process of oral transmission inevitably results in transformation.[88]

Just how radical these transformations can be is best illustrated from a study undertaken in New Mexico amongst the Zuni Indians, which has been recorded by D. Tedlock.[89] The tradition, the creation story of the Zuni, is obviously a religious one. There is no manuscript of the text and the story-teller, Kyaklo, is illiterate. Kyaklo's role in the society is to visit each of the communities once a year to retell the story. Whereas the respect for this sacred story confers on it a certain fixity, the teller is not merely repeating memorized words, nor is it considered a dramatic performance of an established text:

> For the Zuni story teller/interpreter the relationship between text an interpretation is a dialectical one: he or she both respects the text and revises it.[90]

The story-teller not only interprets the tradition but where he or she considers it necessary will improve upon the tradition by adding a scene or answering questions which may be raised in the mind of the story-teller during the process of transmission. The process of recreation of even this sacred religious tradition is quite radical, and at no stage is the transformation due to a lack of memory.

In general, although memory can play a role in oral transmission, it is not as binding as was once thought. The elements of transformation and recreation are far more important aspects of the process.

It has frequently been maintained that the writing down of a tradition will bring to an end the oral process.[91] Yet this is too simplistic an understanding, for studies have shown that a written tradition can co-exist alongside its oral tradition. With reference to

2. Folk Narrative: Its Composition and Transmission

the ballad, Finnegan has provided a number of examples where oral transmission variants persist even though there is a written text.[92] She goes on to suggest:

> In all cases of claimed 'oral transmission'... we need to ask whether writing might not also have played a part in the transmission.[93]

It would seem, therefore, that no general rules of oral transmission can be promulgated. Furthermore, once given a written text it is almost impossible to ascertain with any exactitude which traditions were and which were not transmitted orally. What is clear, however, is that word-for-word memorization of a fixed oral tradition does not occur. Indeed, the concept of a fixed oral tradition is a contradiction in terms.

In his attempt to relate the findings of folklorists more specifically to the biblical text, R.C. Culley argued that whereas oral transmission was often very flexible, it did not mean that the process itself was one of free improvisation.[94] In spite of Culley's remarks it would seem that the role played by improvisation is far greater than we had once thought. The talented story-teller may rely on certain formulae or stock scenes, and use these as 'building blocks', but this is not an adequate means of establishing the relative fixity of a given tradition. Nor can the existence of such building blocks be used to distinguish between oral and written compositions. In his study of parallel stories in the Old Testament, Culley attempted to determine the degree to which these stories reflected oral as opposed to written composition characteristics by employing the concept of stock scenes and episodes, drawn from folklore studies. This study was marred by the paucity of comparative narrative material in the Old Testament. He did, however, suggest the possibility that at least some of the stories in the Old Testament were composed on the basis of a common core of episodes, stereotyped language and expressions. His results were largely negative, however, when it came to determining which texts were the result of oral as opposed to written compositions. Culley also stated that, given the relative proximity of the biblical material to 'a period of traditional oral literature', it might still reflect the influences of oral tradition. He suggested that:

> as the movement away from the oral increases or new genres come into existence in written tradition, the gap between oral style and written style becomes greater.[95]

That Culley should revert to these categories in his conclusions is surprising, since in the rest of his work he has demonstrated his awareness of the difficulties of establishing clear-cut distinctions between oral and written tradition.

3. Implications for the Study of the Patriarchal Narratives in the Old Testament

On the evidence provided by recent folklorists, it is clear that the rules which not only in the past but even today are appealed to for determining oral as opposed to written composition and transmission are untenable. The text of the patriarchal narratives in its present form can provide no absolute grounds for assuming an original oral source.

This has inevitable implications for the possibility of reconstructing a so-called 'patriarchal age', located in Israel's pre-monarchic history. If a study of the pre-literary stage of the material is to be undertaken, other criteria must be appealed to or new methods devised. Are we then driven back to the conclusion of Wellhausen, namely, that in spite of the possibility that some of these stories might have had a pre-literary history, we are unable to rediscover their earlier form?

This question cannot be answered without reference to the much wider issue of the genre classification of these narratives.

Chapter 3

FOLKLORE STUDIES AND THE GENRE OF THE PATRIARCHAL NARRATIVES

1. *'Verbal Art' and the Classification of Written Prose Narrative*

In Chapter 2 it was suggested that our understanding of how folk narratives were composed and transmitted is inextricably bound up with our perception of the genre of these narratives.[1] Of course the issue of genre classification is a central one for form critics who were themselves dependent in large part upon the work of the brothers Grimm for their classifications.[2] We have seen that one of the presuppositions of biblical critics has been the assumption that oral forms of prose narratives are chronologically older than their written counterparts. If a written narrative could be shown to approximate to the form of its presumed oral precursor then it was reasonable to argue that the extant version had had a prior transmission history at the oral stage. The means of identifying the oral precursor, however, have proved to be less satisfactory than was once thought. Suggested ways of distinguishing between oral and written narratives of the same genre have proved generally unsuccessful.

The modern study of folk narrative began with the work of the brothers Grimm. As a result of their research, prose narratives were categorized according to similar patterns of form, content, and context. In the attempt to isolate those units which might have originated in oral composition, it was perhaps inevitable that the stories collected by the brothers Grimm would be compared with the written texts of ancient cultures. As we have seen, the main impetus for such comparisons within biblical studies came from Gunkel, who attempted to isolate the original oral legends in the written text. But it was not only an appeal to similarities between oral and written legends which has been used by scholars to prove the original poetic form of Genesis. Although Gunkel argued against the original poetic form of Genesis,[3] he still referred to it as having a certain poetic quality.[4] More recently F.M. Cross, whilst making no overt reference to the work of Parry and Lord, nonetheless consciously or unconsciously is dependent upon their results when he asserts that behind Genesis lies an epic and oral source.[5] Although this chapter will deal in general with oral genres and their bearing on the written text, both the legend and the epic will receive special attention.[6]

a. *Genre Classification*
The form we give to our verbal expressions can condition the response which they evoke. Consequently, it is important to try to distinguish between forms in order to understand the message each is conveying. The genre categories of myth, legend, and folktale may all be prose narrative communications which attempt to tell a story of one kind or another, but the reality they convey, and therefore the meaning of their message and how it will be heard, will differ. Consequently it is important to understand the elements which distinguish one genre from another:

> We point to genres because by naming certain patterns of expression we are able to talk about the traditional forms and the conventional contents of artistic representation, as well as the patterns of expectation which both the artist and the audience carry into the aesthetic transaction.[7]

Each society has its own genres, its own ways of communicating. Historically,

> les genres mettent en évidence les traits constitutifs de la société à laquelle ils appartiennent.[8]

For T. Todorov, all genres were originally speech acts. The fact that not all speech acts have produced literary genres is because the society chooses and codifies only those speech acts which support its dominant ideology.[9] But how much do we know about the historical evolution of genres?

Despite the attempts of folklorists for more than a century to identify the specific aspects of various narrative genres, A. Dundes, reporting on the state of genre studies in 1964, could nonetheless declare that, 'thus far in the illustrious history of the discipline not so much as one genre has been completely defined'.[10] More recently,

3. Folklore Studies and the Patriarchal Narratives 75

S.K.D. Stahl has argued that clear-cut distinctions between genres cannot be made and that genre categories are but scholarly constructs of ideal types.[11] Since the brothers Grimm the need to establish a classification system has always been considered the initial step of any literary study. In the twentieth century the work of S. Thompson, V. Propp, C.W. von Sydow, A. Jolles and K. Ranke was devoted to establishing just such a system. Yet whereas for folklorists such as the brothers Grimm, S. Thompson, and V. Propp, folklore genres were permanent forms which remained unaffected by evolutionary tendencies, for A. Jolles and K. Ranke genre categories did reflect developmental stages, either in the history of civilization (so Jolles) or of human psychology (so Ranke). Both these approaches have had a significant influence on biblical studies and it will therefore be necessary to discuss them in more detail. Before this can be done, however, the question of terminology needs to be explored, particularly with reference to the German word *Sage*.

b. *Sage/Saga/Legend/Legende*

Before arriving at a cross-discipline consensus on genre definitions, certain problems of translation and therefore terminology must be clarified with respect to the German term *Sage*. The difficulties involved in translating *Sage* into English have long been recognized. Frequently biblical scholars have translated *Sage* as saga.[12] W.H. Carruth's translation of Gunkel's introduction to his commentary on Genesis, and W.F. Albright's subsequent criticism of Carruth's translating *Sage* as legend, is typical of the confusion.[13] When *Sage* is translated into English by the word saga (itself an Icelandic word) two quite different meanings have been assigned to it. The first, which the *Oxford English Dictionary*[14] considers 'correct', is used by T.M. Anderson to mean any written, 'extended novel-like prose narrative dating from the medieval period', Icelandic or otherwise.[15] A second common definition, and one which is described by the *OED* as 'incorrect', is a story which is considered to have some basis in truth about a period which antedates written records and therefore was transmitted orally.[16]

The term legend is frequently used to translate *Sage*, but this can be confusing since legend is often a form-critical category in its own right, designating stories concerning the lives of saints.[17] The situation is further exacerbated by the French translation of *Sage* as *légende*.[18]

A. Olrik's article 'Epische Gesetze der Volksdichtung' muddied the water even further when it used *Sage* as a term which encompassed all oral narrative genres. That Gunkel then proceeded to apply Olrik's conclusions to substantiate his claims was a serious methodological flaw, not least because whereas for Gunkel the term *Sage* was a specific genre category, for Olrik the term was an all-inclusive designation for oral prose narratives of every kind. The very traits which for Gunkel distinguished the legend from other categories of narrative were for Olrik characteristics which pertained to all folk narratives.

In the light of all this, it is no wonder that the various translations have both reflected and compounded such terminological confusion. To make matters worse, all too often scholars have assumed a common use of the terminology where no such agreement exists within the same discipline, let alone across disciplines. This becomes evident once we see how the self-same terminology, far from providing a unified language of scholarly discourse, has become a hidden stumbling-block, since it has no agreed meaning. There is therefore good reason to attempt a brief historical survey of the definitions assigned to folklore genres, so that the situation is clarified when we come to examine the influence folklore genre classifications have had on biblical studies. Since 'legend' is always used by folklorists to translate *Sage*, I have adopted it as well in order to preclude the further confusion which would arise from an interdisciplinary study.

c. *Prose Narrative Categories*
The modern study of folklore genres was carried out by the brothers Grimm during the first half of the nineteenth century. Although they included other genres in their study, the three main categories of prose narrative were myth (*Mythus*), legend (*Sage*), and folktale (*Märchen*). This threefold division is reflected in the three major publications of their folk narrative collections: *Kinder- und Hausmärchen*,[19] *Deutsche Sagen*,[20] and *Deutsche Mythologie*.[21] The distinctive differences between these categories can be seen quite clearly even by a cursory look at the different kinds of narratives in these three collections. In the introduction to *Deutsche Mythologie* J. Grimm offered the following distinctions:

> The Fairy-tale (*Märchen*) is with good reason distinguished from the Legend, though by turns they play into one another. Looser,

3. Folklore Studies and the Patriarchal Narratives 77

less fettered than legend, the Fairy-tale lacks that local habitation which hampers legend, but makes it more home-like. The Fairytale flies, the legend walks, knocks at your door; the one can draw freely out of the fulness of poetry, the other has almost the authority of history. As the Fairy-tale stands related to legend so does legend to history, and (we may add) so does history to real life. In real existence all the outlines are sharp, clear and certain, which on history's canvas are gradually shaded off and toned down. The ancient mythus, however, combines to some extent the qualities of fairy-tale and legend; untrammelled in its flight, it can yet settle down in a local home... In the Fairy-tale also, dwarfs and giants play their part... Fairy-tales, not legends, have in common with the god-myth (*Göttermythus*) a multitude of metamorphoses; and they often let animals come upon the stage, and so they trespass on the old animal-epos... Divinities form the core of all mythology.[22]

While lacking the precision some would like, these distinctions remained operative until the turn of the century, when scholars attempted new and more precise criteria for genre distinctions. When reading the collection it is easy to forget how much of an editorial process they have undergone. Recently the re-publication of the 1810 manuscript of *Kinder- und Hausmärchen* along with the 1812 edition of the tales has shown the extent of the alterations which were made to the former. J. Zipes has provided examples of this editorial process, tracing the amendments through three successive editions in an attempt to analyze the significance of the changes:

> We can see how each and every oral tale was conscientiously and, at times, drastically changed by the Grimms... The changes in the versions reveal social transitions and class differences which attest to their dependency on the gradual ascendancy of bourgeois codes and tastes.[23]

Even the few examples which Zipes presents in order to illustrate the influence of the brothers Grimm on the material, are sufficient warning against using these collections as the basis for establishing possible indicators of orality. Furthermore, whereas present-day folklore studies have emphasized the importance of the narrator of a tale, Zipe's comparisons point out just how significant the role of the collector and transcriber can be:

> Consciously and unconsciously the Grimms integrated their world into the tales and those of their intended audience as well.[24]

That the work of the brothers Grimm has been extremely influential in shaping our own attitudes to folk narrative compositions is self-evident. But that the degree of their editorial reworking of the tales was so extensive is not always acknowledged. The idea that these tales are the distillation of oral narratives told by country peasants is still a widely held view, as Zipe's work has shown. In fact they are no such thing, and should not be used as examples of typical folk compositions. The literary nature of these tales and the influence exerted on them by the brothers Grimm should be stressed.[25] That some of the original tales were oral is not disputed, but their final form cannot be taken as reflecting typical folk narrative. In J.M. Ellis's study of the brothers Grimm and the editorial processes involved in *Kinder- und Hausmärch* it is made abundantly clear that the stories are far from typical folk narrative. The Grimms' editing was no minor alteration in style and language, but the gradual imposition of a uniformity absent from the original stories. Thus,

> a predominant 'voice' of the stories was cultivated, and stock figures, situations and motifs progressively emerge.[26]

The voice was not that of the typical German peasant but of the brothers Grimm. Although they claimed to preserve the national speech of the people they had in reality imposed their own *Schriftsprache*.[27] There were seven editions of the *Kinder- und Hausmärchen* and with the exception of the seventh all of them represented major revisions.[28]

Finally, it is now clear that the Grimms' sources were not older, unlettered 'German peasant transmitters of an indigenous oral tradition' but rather highly educated young middle-class and literate acquaintances.[29] Whatever else they may be used for, these tales cannot be used to substantiate the forms of oral traditional narratives.

In 1908 G.L. Gomme, while outlining some of the problems of definition, complained that terms such as myth, legend and folktale were being used indiscriminately with little attempt to delineate their differences. Retaining the same terminology, Gomme defined myth in terms of its origins in the 'most primitive stages of human thought'. It functioned as an explanation of some natural phenomenon, some forgotten or unknown object of human origin or some event of lasting influence. The folktale was a survival of an older age than the one in which it was preserved, and dealt 'with events and ideas of primitive times in terms of the experience of episodes in the lives of unnamed human beings'. The legend was defined by Gomme as being 'attached to an historical personage, locality or event'.[30] The significant difference in these definitions is one which centres on the notion of historicity. Whereas J.L.C. Grimm had been sufficiently vague on the matter, for Gomme the difference between legend and the other two categories of myth and folktale was one of historicity.

Frazer's attempts to define these three terms resemble those of Gomme, although Frazer suggested that the legend contained a mixture of truth and falsehood. Myths were mistaken explanations of natural phenomena which a more advanced society would explain by means of philosophy and science. Folktales were fictitious narratives composed by unknown persons and transmitted orally, their sole purpose being one of entertainment, whereas legends were either oral or written narratives about 'real people in the past' or described 'events not necessarily human' but which had taken place at 'real places'. Elements 'of the marvellous or the miraculous' entered into them, which meant that they contained 'a mixture of truth and falsehood'.[31] Both Gomme and Frazer, however, hardly advanced the discussion of genre distinctions.

In a detailed study of one sub-category of the folktale, V. Propp provided a morphological analysis of the fairy tale.[32] Using examples from a collection of Russian fairy tales (*skazki*), Propp showed that each tale comprised a certain number of functions, or actions, which could be performed by a variety of *dramatis personae*. Each function followed the other in a fixed pattern. Propp identified thirty-one functions and the sequence of these functions constituted the morphology of the tale, or the way the tale was composed.[33] Each fairy tale in the corpus when analysed followed the same skeletal outline and had the same structure. Thus, Propp provided a different way of identifying the salient characteristics of a fairy tale in terms of structure as opposed to content. Presumably it could be possible to analyse other folktale types on the same basis, to see whether or not they too followed certain universal structural laws of composition. Indeed it might even be possible to establish a system of functions which operated for other folk narrative genres, such as legends, myths or riddles.

One of the problems of applying this particular system to the biblical narrative is the very paucity of stories which could be identified as folktales, a problem which will be dealt with in relation to the work of H. Jason.[34] The one attempt which has been made to isolate certain types of folktales in the Jacob narratives of Genesis from a structuralist perspective has been that of R. Barthes.[35] Taking Gen. 32.23-33 as a folktale, Barthes demonstrates how it fulfils certain functions which are identified as typical of the folktale. It achieves its effect, however, by the very fact that the resolution of the tale contravenes the normally accepted rules of folktale composition. It is precisely the breaking of these rules which lends a uniqueness to the Old Testament literature. In the case of Genesis 32 the rules are not followed, in that Jacob's struggle with the messenger at the Jabbok turns out to be a struggle with God. But in the structural analysis of the fairy tale the originator of the quest and the opponent of the quest cannot be one and the same character. It is precisely this structural difference which allows Barthes to arrive at certain theological motivations for the story, which, although interesting, are not pertinent to this discussion. He argues that in this instance the literary form constitutes a defence of monotheism, precisely because it does not follow the expected rules, i.e. the originator of the quest and the opponent are God. Therefore the narrative cannot be considered as a true fairy tale, and therein lies its power.

One of the real problems confronting any study of Old Testament narratives is that the number of examples of any particular genre is so limited. It is probably this factor more than any other which restricts clear-cut conclusions of such an approach as Barthes'. What has yet to be proved is that the ancient Near East was sufficiently conscious of the fairy tale as a genre to exploit it in this way. As an interpretation of the present-day reader's expectations it may be valid, but unless it can be shown that such a technique was used in other instances it can provide no useful insights into either (a) how biblical folktales in general were composed or (b) the structures of the society which composed them. Furthermore, the development and successful application of Propp's methods to other genres has been limited. The one notable exception has been the work of A. Dundes, who analysed a number of oral North American traditions.[36] The results of Dundes' study would seem to imply that there is a universality of form which remains unaffected by cultural or historical contingencies. In the case of Pentikäinen's analysis of Marina Takalo's fairy tales, only certain kinds were amenable to Propp's scheme. In general the insights of Propp were unhelpful, and

3. Folklore Studies and the Patriarchal Narratives

frequently contradicted his own analysis.[37] The relevance of such work for the understanding of how biblical narratives were composed and their meaning has still to be proved.

In so far as Propp's work argued that genres could be identified by their form, it implied that there were universal rules which governed their composition. Propp's approach was in many respects in opposition to the theoretical work of A. Jolles. As we have already observed, his *Einfache Formen* published in 1929[38] has had, and is still having, a substantial influence on Old Testament studies, mainly through the work of C. Westermann.[39]

Jolles attempted to establish the primary or simple literary forms of various narrative genres, in order to trace how they developed into more complex forms:

> Die Literaturwissenschaft ist dreifach gerichtet. In einer etwas abgegriffenen Terminologie heisst: sie besitzt eine ästhetische, eine historische und eine morphologische Aufgabe.[40]

For Jolles, given certain conditions and situations language has an inherent ability to transfer into forms which reflect the given situation. This process is itself a basic mental activity. As these words begin to take form they do so around certain distinct fields of meaning. A genre can and does frequently transform itself into a more complex form. Nevertheless this more complex type will still correspond in meaning to the earlier form. These primary forms of language can be isolated as follows:

> Formen, die weder von der Stilistik, noch von der Rhetorik, noch von der Poetik, ja, vielleicht nicht einmal von der 'Schrift' erfasst werden, die, obwohl sie zur Kunst gehören nicht eigentlich zum Kunstwerk werden, die, wenn auch Dichtung, so doch keine Gedichte darstellen kurz... Formen, die man als Legende, Sage, Mythe, Rätsel, Spruch, Kasus, Memorabile, Märchen, oder Witz zu bezeichnen pflegt.[41]

It is his work on the category of legend (*Sage*) which has had the most influence on studies of the patriarchal narratives. In an attempt to define *Sage* Jolles quotes the definition found in Grimm's dictionary, which states that *Sage* signifies:

> 1. Im Sinne von Sprache Fähigkeit zu sprechen, Tätigkeit des Sprechens.
> 2. Das was gesagt wird in allgemeiner Anwendung: Ausspruch, Mitteilung, Aussage usw. und dann in besonderer Wendung eine

Aussage vor Gericht, ein urkundliches Zeugnis, eine Prophezeiung usw.[42]

Not satisfied with either of these statements Jolles turned to the *Oxford English Dictionary* where he noted the two definitions (already cited on p. 75), one correct and the other incorrect:

> Das Englische kennt das Wort Sage nicht, wohl aber 'Saga'. 1. any of the narrative compositions in prose that were written in Iceland or Norway during the middle ages. Danach 1b. übertragen: a narrative having the (real or supposed) characteristics of the Icelandic sagas.
> 2. in incorrect uses (partly as the equivalent of the cognate German *Sage*) a story popularly believed to be a matter of fact, which has been developed by gradual accretions in course of ages, and has been handed down by oral tradition; historical or heroic legend as distinguished both from authentic history and from intentional fiction.[43]

Jolles accepted this distinction, and whilst he relied on the first definition for the term *Sage*, he nonetheless maintained that Icelandic Sagas had originated as oral compositions. Although these oral forms no longer existed, they had been preserved in the written text.

Jolles identified three separate groups of Icelandic sagas:

> Wir nennen die erste Gruppe Islendiga sogur (sogur von Isländern), die zweite Koninga sogur (sogur von Königen), die dritte Fronalder sogur (sogur aus der alten Zeit).[44]

Of these three the family sagas were the oldest, and therefore it is the situation of the family which is needed to create the necessary mental activity which produces the saga. Taking a simple developmental approach to the history of civilization, Jolles went on to argue that this situation precedes the development of the state:

> Aus dieser Vergegenwärtigung können wir die formgebende Geistesbeschäftigung und ihre Gedankengänge ablesen und erfassen. Bei der Sage deuten wir die Geistesbeschäftigung mit den Kennworten Familie, Stämme, Blutsverwandtschaften.[45]

So, as a simple form, the saga is created within the situation of the family and therefore reflects typical familial concerns. As one of his examples Jolles chooses to compare the patriarchal narratives with those concerning David. Both are narratives set within families and

3. Folklore Studies and the Patriarchal Narratives 83

both span several generations. However, what distinguishes the two is the fact that the patriarchal narratives are not so much concerned with affairs of state as with strictly family matters:

> Ich möchte, da ich auch hier nicht beabsichtige, eine Geschichte der Sage zu geben, auf die israelitische Sage nicht weiter eingehen. Ich verweise nur einerseits auf die Ereignisse aus der Sage der Erzväter, der Patriarchen und andererseits auf das, was sich in dem Hause Davids begibt und was im 2 Samuelis und 1 Könige erzählt wird. Wir finden wieder bei einer Vergleichbarkeit des Stoffes eine völlige Unvergleichbarkeit der Geisteseinstellung, der Geistesbeschäftigung, und wir sehen, dass die Form, aus der sich die Patriarchen und ihre Nachkommen ergeben, eine andere ist als die Form, in der Konigssöhne zu Davids Zeit lebten und erlebt wurden. Hier wird die Familiengeschichte, die Königsfrage vom Staate Israel aus gedeutet.[46]

Thus from nine finite forms (religious legend, saga, myth, riddle, proverb, lawsuit, memoirs, folktales and jokes) all written literature evolved. These forms first appeared amongst the most primitive of peoples in ancient times, and although they have evolved into more complex forms they still retain the same field of meaning. For Jolles they are the verbal forms of our mental attitudes which are formed and shaped according to the environment we inhabit.

Jolles' thesis however has never gained acceptance amongst folklorists, largely because he paid so little attention to known oral genres.[47] Whereas scholarly opinion in the nineteenth century accepted the Icelandic sagas as written versions of fixed oral compositions, such theories have long since had to undergo considerable modification. The debate has prompted the suggestion that these sagas were the creations of literary genius. Consequently, for lack of any evidence of the orality of the original composition the historicity of their contents is now almost completely denied, or at best ignored.[48] The present state of scholarship in the area of Icelandic family saga composition is more non-committal and prefers the somewhat

> vague formulation that the sagas are based on pre-existing stories and pre-existing narrative modes, but that the shape in which they have come down to us is the work of man making the transition from oral narrative to literary composition.[49]

The critique of Jolles' position offered by von Sydow was also significant. Von Sydow maintained that a more complex classification system was needed. He also criticized Jolles' unscientific methods in differentiating between the legend (*Sage*) and the folktale (*Märchen*).[50] Finally, Jolles was criticized for introducing a metaphysic which placed his thesis beyond the realms of verifiable proof.[51]

In spite of these serious criticisms of his work, Jolles' conclusions have been utilized by biblical scholars. The fact that they were never accepted by folklorists does not of itself invalidate his position, but it should warn us against accepting his theories too uncritically.

In the case of C. Westermann, the use of Jolles' understanding of saga is central to his own thesis concerning the patriarchal narratives. Westermann chooses not to use the designation saga for the stories in Genesis because in German they are too often confused with hero legend (*Heldensage*). Instead he employs the term narrative (*Erzählung*). Jolles' analogy between Icelandic family sagas and the patriarchal narratives provides Westermann with the original Sitz im Leben of the narratives. Since their concerns are completely familial, like the Icelandic family sagas the patriarchal narratives originated within the confines of the family unit. Historically, such a situation pre-dates the establishment of a state. Indeed according to Jolles the family saga is one of the earliest of these primary forms to emerge.

> The patriarchal stories are thus concerned with the life of the family and clan and therefore 'deal with a private or circumstantial domain'.[52]

Given Jolles' description of Icelandic Sagas, when compared with the other Genesis narratives the patriarchal stories evidently antedate those of Genesis 1–11.

Westermann also maintained that the promise motif was not always secondary. It was precisely in the family narratives that the motif proved to be part of the narrative itself.[53] Thus, narratives which originated at a time when the family unit was the primary sociological institution were handed down by oral transmission and only later, during the monarchy, were they given written expression. From what period did they originate? Westermann does not want to commit himself to an absolute date. However, he suggests that these family narratives reflect a period before the exodus and the settlement of the tribes in Canaan:

> I agree with the archaeological approach in that the study of the world of the patriarchs has shown the possibility of patriarchal life

3. *Folklore Studies and the Patriarchal Narratives* 85

and movement for the period before the Exodus and before the settlement of the tribes in Canaan... a period for which fixed dates cannot be given.[54]

Furthermore, it is within the family that the oral transmission of these narratives took place,[55] handed down from one generation to the next until by the time of the kings these family narratives took on a national significance.[56] Finally, by using Jolles' Icelandic analogy Westermann suggests that the Icelandic king sagas are best represented in the Old Testament by the narratives in Judges. We have already seen, however, that the likelihood of such a long transmission period preserving the ancient primary form of a narrative cannot be maintained. Furthermore, it is not generally agreed that such primary forms should be viewed in historico-developmental terms. So, for example, K. Ranke argued that Jolles' primary forms were the outcome of certain universal psychological needs. These go back to the beginning of human existence and have persisted up to the present. Consequently these primary forms do not necessarily develop into more complex ones, but maintain their simple structures.[57] This position would of course completely undermine Westermann's thesis. On these grounds Westermann's dating of the patriarchal narratives cannot be maintained. Nor can their familial interests be used to demonstrate their primacy.

Apart from the theoretical concerns of Jolles and Rank, folklorists in the period between 1930 and 1960 were engaged in attempts to refine the distinctions between folk narratives. C.W. von Sydow proceeded to subdivide the larger categories of myth, legend and folktale into subtypes or regional 'oikotypes' which he considered possessed their own separate histories. In reaction to the Finnish school's comparative methods, von Sydow argued that oral tales developed their own regional characteristics as they spread from one area to another. Whereas the Finnish school maintained that tale variants were caused by the diffusion of tales and that the original form could be found, von Sydow argued that each 'oikotype' possessed its own individual history. The tracing of tale type migration was therefore an impossible venture. The age of the original tale was impossible to arrive at.[58]

It had been through the previous efforts of A. Aarne and S. Thompson (both members of the Finnish school) that an index of folktale types had been compiled. Thompson followed this up with the *Motif Index of Folk Literature*, an index which sought to catalogue the various motifs to be found in traditional literature, oral or written.[59] His definitions for the various categories of folk narrative were worked out in his book *The Folktale*. Thompson used the term 'folktale' as an all-inclusive term for the 'forms of prose narrative, written or oral, which have come to be handed down through the years'.[60] He retained the German term *Märchen* and defined it as a tale of some length which would incorporate a number of motifs or episodes occurring in the unreal world at unspecified locations.[61] Similarly, he retained the German term *Sage* for legend and described it as having a simple structure which would normally only contain one single narrative motif, purporting to tell the story of an extraordinary event in history. Although the *Sage* attached itself to a particular locality, it could nonetheless transfer itself to different places. Often it told of encounters with marvellous creatures in which the people believed.[62] Closely related to this was the aetiological tale, which, while having its own existence as a tale, could be attached to any narrative form.

Although Thompson provided these distinctions he nonetheless argued that the form of these categories was very much less stable than the plot structure, and that the different categories tended to blend with one another with great facility.[63] Thus Thompson could conclude that historico-geographic studies as practised by the Finnish school were concerned primarily with the content and therefore the plot of the tale and not its form. For Thompson the form had little importance for the history of any one tale.[64]

This reluctance to define narratives in terms of their form was paralleled in Old Testament studies during this period. Certainly Eissfeldt's distinction between *Märchen* and *Sage* is based solely on content.[65] Both deal with the marvellous and are only meant to entertain. They are therefore to be distinguished from historical narratives.[66] They are the product of oral narration, whereas historical narratives are the product of writing and, therefore, the educated classes.[67] There can be no historical reflection without writing. Even so, Eissfeldt considered the patriarchal legends to be tribal histories. Unlike Gunkel, who thought the narratives had their origin in *Märchen* to which only later historiographic elements were added, Eissfeldt considered the narratives to have originated as legends of individual ancestors who subsequently became representatives of the community.[68] This shift from ancestor legend to tribal and national legend resulted in certain modifications in the

3. Folklore Studies and the Patriarchal Narratives

narrative detail. In transmission the original historical context was lost, and their focus became centred on the circumstances and characteristics of the individual. Thereby these original heroes became identified with certain universal attributes which transcended the exigencies of time.[69] In some of the legends the historical elements had been preserved and were central to the narrative, whereas in others they had receded into the background and been submerged under later literary and imaginative elaboration. Whereas for Gunkel the stealing of the blessing by Jacob in Genesis 27 had originated as a folktale and only subsequently had historical reminiscences been attached to it, for Eissfeldt these historical reminiscences have been supplanted by an imaginative literary construct whch has placed the ancestor into the family setting with which all the people can identify. In the one case we have the gradual historicizing of a folktale; in the other imaginative accretions obscure the historical tribal legend, since past events are always modified in the light of modern circumstances.[70] Those elements in the extant story which originated during the pre-settlement period have been modified to reflect the concerns and circumstances of the period in which they were written down. But what is the criterion for distinguishing the original historical elements from later literary constructs? Certainly if the original intention of the tales was historical and if historical elements can be gleaned from the text, then the transmission history must be shorter than Eissfeldt allowed for.

Recognizing the need for generally agreed definitions and terms in the field of folklore, W.R. Bascom has stated:

> It is time to agree upon English equivalents of *Mythen*, *Sagen* and *Märchen*, and to agree upon their definitions.[71]

To this end Bascom proposed the following equivalents and definitions:

> *Folktales are prose narratives which are regarded as fiction.* They are not considered as dogma or history. They may or may not have happened and they are not to be taken seriously... they are not only told for amusement... as the class of moral folktales should have suggested... they are almost timeless and placeless. They have been called 'nursery tales' but in many societies they are not restricted to children. They have also been known as 'fairy tales' but this is inappropriate both because narratives about fairies are

usually regarded as true and because fairies do not appear in most folktales. Fairies, ogres and even deities may appear but folktales usually recount the adventures of animal or human characters.

Myths are prose narratives which in the society in which they are told are considered to be truthful accounts of what happened in the remote past. They are accepted on faith: they are taught to be believed; . . . they are usually sacred. Their main characters are not usually human beings, but they often have human attributes; they are animal deities or culture heroes, whose actions are set in an earlier world when the earth was different from what it is today or in another world such as the sky or underworld. Myths account for the origin of the world of mankind of death or for characteristics of birds, animals, geographical features and the phenomena of nature. They may recount the activities of the deities. They may purport to explain details . . . but such etiological elements are not confined to myths.

Legends are prose narratives which like myths are regarded as true by the narrator and his audience but they are set in a period considered less remote when the world was much as it is today. Legends are more often secular than sacred and their principal characters are human. They tell of migrations, wars and victories, deeds of past heroes, chiefs and kings and succession in ruling dynasties. In this they are often the counterpart in verbal tradition of written history, but they also include local tales of buried treasure, ghosts and saints.[72]

In the same article Bascom proceeded to analyse a plethora of stories from different societies, namely the Ashanti, Yoruba, Kimbundu, and Fon of Africa, the Marshall, the Trobriand Islanders, and the Fulani, and from North America the Mandan Hidatsa, and Arikara, in order to test the universal applicability of his definitions. On his own admission, however, his tripartite division is not to be found in all societies. Some do not distinguish between myths and legends but place them all into the same category, one which is only distinguished from folktale in terms of belief.

One of the major concerns in more recent folklore studies has been the performance aspect of story-telling and its relation to genre classification. The mood of both the story-teller and the audience has been analysed to see whether or not a particular style is adopted by the narrator according to the particular genre. So R. Finnegan in her work on the Limba people argued that although the narrators did not

3. *Folklore Studies and the Patriarchal Narratives* 89

differentiate between stories in terms of formal analytical genre categories, nevertheless distinctions were made in terms of how and when certain stories were told. With the Limba people the manner of differentiation was determined behaviourally, in terms of their response to the performance.[73] Further investigation has led scholars such as L. Dégh and G. Ortutay to stress the collective nature of folktale composition, arguing that narrators are influenced by their audience and will alter their narratives accordingly. Thus the audience becomes an active participant in the creation of variants. Recognizing the context as having a formidable influence on the way certain narratives are classified R. Abrahams has stated:

> the central focus of the structure of context is on the performer-audience relations. It is here for instance that we make our distinctions among the major folkloristic genres of myth, legend and folktale, for the difference pointed to in these fictive forms is one of level of belief. This has to do with the way in which the audience apprehends the tone of the performer and interprets his meaning.[74]

Recently the attempts by Bascom to arrive at universally agreed genre categories has come under criticism from D. Ben-Amos. These criticisms are worth mentioning here since they have implications for any future attempt to utilize the genre classifications of folklore narrative in the biblical field.

Ben-Amos has maintained that folklore communication is based upon culturally determined rules and therefore what is needed are studies of ethnic systems of genre classification. Bascom's tripartite system of genres does not allow for the complexity of different ethnic genres.[75] Observing that Bascom himself had difficulties in applying his classification transculturally, Ben-Amos has argued that differences in names of genres and their meanings reflect cultural idiosyncrasies. Thus,

> Deciphering their significance may provide us with the key for understanding folklore communication the way its speakers do.[76]

Consequently, Ben-Amos rejects all attempts to construct analytical categories of genre classification which can be applied transculturally:

> the study of the ethnic system of genres must combine the cognitive expressive and behavioural levels of genres in each

> ... If folklore communication ... is based upon culturally
> rules then their discovery is essential. The system of genres
> rimary ethnic formulation of such a grammar of folklore.[77]

If the criteria for genre classification are so culturally bound,[78] it would appear that the discipline of folklore genre research can be of little use to Old Testament studies. Furthermore, most folklorists are now agreed that the only element which distinguishes between genres both in popular and high art is the aspect of performance. Therefore the context in which a certain narrative is told, very often affects its genre category.[79] The form and content of different genres are variable. The same story may realize itself in different genres, and therefore 'what is a tale for one culture may be an origin legend for another'.[80] Finally, the importance of context should not be underestimated:

> Rooted in their social environment stories are extremely sensitive to group and individual attitudes; the greater their popularity, the greater their inconsistency. They have no 'final' form.[81]

2. Folk Narrative and the Biblical Text

If the performance aspect of oral composition and transmission is the final determining factor for genre categories then it can have very little relevance for the study of written texts. In other words it is necessary to make a distinction between oral and written genres. A particular written form may have similar features to its oral counterpart, but without the aspect of performance it loses an essential characteristic which prevents us from viewing 'the forms of verbal art the way native speakers do'.[82] Whereas this may be pertinent to the study of present-day folk traditions, the genres biblical scholars deal with have achieved a 'frozen state' by virtue of their written form. Although Gunkel attempted to isolate their salient characteristics and compare them with those of later narrative forms such as the folktale and the legend, this was inadequate for establishing the original oral composition.[83]

Recently the work of D. Irvin[84] has yielded some interesting results in the area of biblical prose narrative analysis, by utilizing S. Thompson's *Motif Index of World Folklore*. Irvin's aim was to isolate and identify not the motifs found in ancient Near Eastern texts, but rather the 'plot motifs' which are similar to those in certain designated messenger stories in Genesis. For Irvin a plot motif is an element within the plot which moves the story forward a step, and constitutes one type of motif found within the Motif Index.[85] In addition to successfully isolating certain motifs which the literatures of the ancient Near East have in common Irvin also attempted to single out typical 'traditional episodes' which she argued were analogous to Parry's formulaic phrases and epithets. On the basis of these traditional episodes she concluded that many of the ancient Near Eastern texts were oral in character:

> The 'episode' functions like a Homeric epithet in that it is so highly standardized that the story reaches a point at which an episode tells itself, so to speak, and leaves the story teller's mind free to think ahead and plan the next part of the story.[86]

Yet as we have seen, the appeal to the presence of formulaic language and/or traditional episodes is not a legitimate way to establish a text's original oral form,[87] and therefore whilst Irvin's comparisons are interesting,[88] they should not be used as proof of oral composition. However Irvin's study not only provides a useful comparative analysis, it also sounds a salutary warning against concluding anything about the possible borrowing of motifs by one culture from another on the basis of such a limited number of examples:

> Literary parallels in the Ancient Near East... seldom contain larger units of similarity than one or two motifs, which they have in common with the folktales of the entire world, or a traditional episode.[89]

This warning is important to keep in mind, especially when dealing with the work of H. Jason, who has attempted to trace the origins of certain folktales found throughout the ancient Near East. Like Thompson, Irvin did not attempt to distinguish between genres but was concerned rather with the plot motifs of folk narrative in general, presumably in an attempt to trace their origins. Because of the lack of material her conclusions in this area were negative.

Jason's work, on the other hand, concentrated on delineating folk genres or, to use her own terminology, 'ethnopoetic genres'. For Jason, 'ethnopoetry' is defined as 'oral literature', which exists only in a performance presented to an audience.[90] Like Ben-Amos, Jason considers every cultural area to have its own repertoire of genres.[91] She argues that since most of the genres existing today in the 'Western Old World' cultures were already present in the cultures of the ancient Near East, they should all be considered as one cultural group designated as Euro-Asian.[92] Nevertheless, it is not the case that all genres will be found in certain areas, and it would therefore

> be a mistake to automatically transfer concepts of ethnopoetic genres developed through the study of European material to other cultural areas.[93]

Jason's classification of genres is the most complete to date and provides a unique way of organizing the material. According to Jason, there are three separate modes in which all genres are realized, i.e.: (i) the fabulous; (ii) the realistic; (iii) the symbolic.[94] In the fabulous mode man confronts the world of the fantastic wherein an amorphous power or various agents of that power manipulate the events of the tale. The two forms of the fabulous are the numinous (itself with three basic manifestations) and the marvellous. The marvellous is confined to a fairy tale land, where the marvellous power bears no relation to the system of societal values and beliefs. It is a world completely unrelated to the laws of nature.[95] In the realist mode man confronts his fellow man in a human world where non-natural elements do not exist. In the symbolic mode the entities are neither real nor fabulous, nor have they any properties but are themselves symbols of properties.[96]

Each of these modes is manifest in various genres and sub-genres. Realistic genres include the novella and all its sub-categories, and the historic song.[97] The genres in the fabulous mode are divided between the genres of the numinous, which include myth, the trickster tale and legend with its sub-categories,[98] and the genres of the marvellous, which include the fairy tale and its sub-genres.[99] The genres in the symbolic mode include the proverb riddle, parable formula tale, tall tale, lying tale, topsy-turvy tale, numskull tale and joke, all of which cannot be placed on the realistic-fabulous axis.[100] Jason considers it impossible to establish which genre had precedence. She does, however, state that in those countries with universal monotheistic religions the genre of myth has ceased to be part of that culture's ethnopoetry.[101]

Jason's system of genre classification is helpful in that it distinguishes between genres as much by form and content as by function. How successful it will be in classifying Euro-Asian tales still needs (on her own admission) to be tested. Recently, however,

3. Folklore Studies and the Patriarchal Narratives   93

she has applied her classificatory system to the biblical text and has reached some singular conclusions. We have already seen that some scholars had maintained that the original form of the Genesis narrative had been that of an epic. So for example F.M. Cross saw behind Genesis an oral tradition composed and transmitted in verse 'designed to recreate and give meaning to the historical expression of a people or nation'.[102] This position was never substantiated by Cross, however; he simply asserted that the Pentateuchal narrative JE was first composed as an epic.[103] Since reconstructing that original epic form, or even for that matter attempting to isolate certain features of the epic, has never been attempted, Jason's work on the story of David and Goliath in 1 Samuel 17 might at least have suggested a possible means of establishing the existence of an original verse form of the present text.

To this end Jason uses various techniques.[104] Obviously she is dependent upon her own classificatory sytem for much of the analysis[105] and, as I have stated, this system has yet to be fully tested. I shall therefore concentrate on those other techniques of repetition, parallelism, the epithet and formulaic numbers, which she employs in her attempt to demonstrate the text's oral origins.

Jason states that one of the prominent characteristics of 'epic in verse' is 'repetition of speeches or events in full, in the same or similar wording' and suggests that such repetition is in evidence in 1 Samuel 17. She has proposed that the text consists of two kinds of passages: those which recount the event in detail, and those which summarize the preceding events.[106] Although she has provided a table dividing 1 Samuel 17 into these two categories, it is not entirely clear how she is defining 'repetition'. In what sense is it meaningful to classify vv. 14-16 as a summary of vv. 1-13? Against Jason it can be maintained that, far from merely summarizing the narrative, these verses extend the story line, by providing new information. So we are told not merely the names of the three eldest sons of Jesse, but are given the information that the young David, unlike his brothers, was not in Saul's army but still had to tend his father's herds. This one example is not atypical of the rest of Jason's 'summary repetitions' and calls into question how far the biblical text does in fact fit her description of it.

Jasons's second criterion is that of parallelism. Of this she can, on her own admission, only produce 'two relatively clear' instances, 1 Sam. 17.1 and 1 Sam. 17.52.[107] Relative to what, however, is not so clear. Parallelism is a term which is normally used of 'a type of repetition (usually a binary pattern) in which one element is changed, the other—usually the syntactic frame itself—remains constant'.[108] It is doubtful whether either instance cited by Jason could be classified as an example of parallelism, however. In the light of this, the cases which she cites as 'less evident' examples of parallelism only go to illustrate further the inaccurate way in which she uses the term. For example, it is erroneous to claim parallelism for phrases which are non-consecutive. Yet Jason does so for 1 Sam. 17.8 and 1 Sam. 17.10.

Her search for epithets is also contentious. Jason can only produce four examples of what she calls 'quasi-epithets', only one of which, 'Goliath the Philistine' (1 Sam. 17.23), would be defined as an epithet by others. One's confidence in her attention to the text is even more undermined by the peculiar translation she offers for 1 Sam. 17.45, where she translates 'God of the living Israel' instead of 'God of the armies of Israel'.[109] If, as Jason suggests, a large number of these features are found in the epics of oral societies, she has not shown them to be present in 1 Samuel 17.

To these arguments Jason adds a structural analysis based on the methods of V. Propp and Skaftymor.[110] She maintains that the text is a product of oral literature which is amenable to all the tools of folklore and fulfils the criteria of orality. But we have seen that this text does not lend itself to the folkloristic tools Jason relies upon. With the possible exception of her structural analysis, the tools she has used can offer no assurances of orality.[111] Having said this, I would not want to deny that the rest of Jason's analysis proves the text to be a romantic epic as defined by her own classificatory system.[112] What she has not shown, however, is that the story betrays evidence of an original oral verse form. Repetition, parallelism, and the use of epithets may all indicate possible orality, but in the case of Jason's chosen example, their existence in the text of 1 Samuel 17 on any normally accepted definition of those terms is either negligible or non-existent. More precise examples of these features are needed before a written prose text can be assumed to be masking an original oral verse form. The idea that much of the biblical material was originally composed and transmitted as an epic is fanciful and based on the assumption that oral verse forms are less likely to alter in transmission than oral prose. Until adequate means can be found which will indicate that a given text was formerly an oral and

3. Folklore Studies and the Patriarchal Narratives 95

possibly a poetic composition the term epic should not be used of the biblical text.[113]

Jason's efforts to determine the oral basis of the biblical narratives and ancient Near Eastern literature in general has also been argued in an article she wrote with A. Kempinski entitled 'How Old are Folktales?'[114]

In this article the literature of the ancient Near East has been collected and classified according to Jason's genre categories. The authors have contended that in the ancient Near Eastern world there existed a fully developed sytem of oral tales dating from the second millennium BCE. Whilst conceding that these narratives have not been preserved equally in the writings of these various cultures they nonetheless assert that 'oral tradition did exist in the same measure among all the ancient people'.[115] We may have only remnants of this oral tradition in a few extant texts, but these are sufficient to indicate the existence of a fully developed system of folktales which was 'uniform throughout the Ancient Near East'.[116]

The authors admit that the dating of much of the material is problematic since the extant scribal form is not necessarily the earliest date of a given story. With reference to the biblical material Jason and Kempinski state that although oral tradition existed amongst the Israelite tribes from their nomadic period,[117] the dating of much of the material in the Pentateuch, Joshua, Judges and Samuel can only be calculated from the point when this material was written down, a date which they place between the tenth and sixth centuries BCE. The tenth century is chosen as the earliest date on the basis of various inscriptions which the authors offer as evidence of a widespread literacy.[118] Such literacy, they argue, prevented the development of a 'rigid, closed scribal class'. Indeed the Israelite documentation provides no evidence of such a class. However, the authors do acknowledge that Israel did have scribes of one sort or another and suggest that because they had no written tradition to act as their model they turned to folk tradition. This tradition provided them with the genres of myth, epic and legend, genres which suited their theological purposes as they tell 'true and real history'.[119]

As Jason and Kempinski point out, this obviously has implications for the present-day folklorist, who must now take seriously the fact that a great deal of his materials existed at a far earlier date than had hitherto been supposed. Furthermore, any attempts to trace the historical development of a tale plot on the basis of written texts will now have to be re-evaluated.

If correct, these conclusions will have far-reaching ramifications for the handling of the biblical material, necessitating an analysis which takes into account the oral pre-history of a story and its possible inception in other ancient Near Eastern cultures. But just how valid and accurate are these results? The early date which is suggested for the 'system' is based on the evidence of just four folk narratives. Indeed for the entire period stretching from the second millennium down to the tenth century BCE only twenty-three folk narratives are given as evidence for a complete and universally held system of folk stories.[120] The authors can only make such a claim because of their initial assumption that oral tradition existed in the same measure in each ancient society, even though the texts which would indicate the existence of such an oral literature are not to be found equally among the various cultures of the ancient Near East. The basis for such an assumption is never given, merely the assertion that 'no people on Earth (sic) has been found to lack oral tradition'.[121] True as this statement may be, it does not follow that each culture has had the same extensive body of oral literature. This is not to preclude the possibility that ancient Near Eastern cultures had oral traditions, some of which were shared, thus producing similar stories in different periods and different cultures. This, however, is far removed from a postulated universal system of folk narratives, shared in equal measure by ancient Near Eastern cultures. The proof for such a system has still to be found. All that Jason and Kempinski have shown is that many of our modern genre classifications can be found in the written literature of the ancient Near East.

The extent to which folklore studies have influenced Old Testament genre classification is evident. In many respects the debates within folklore have been mirrored in Old Testament studies. In an attempt to substantiate the claims made by the written text, scholars in both folklore and Old Testament studies created the world of the oral pre-text—a world which had preserved at least some of the memories of our pre-literary and primitive ancestors in the oral tales they had transmitted. The oral genre classifications of the nineteenth and the first half of the twentieth centuries seemed to provide a basis for comparison between oral and written text, i.e. that their resemblances could be attributed to a common original orality. This was a somewhat simplistic view of orality, prompted in large part by the remnants of romantic theory. Obviously there are texts which do

3. Folklore Studies and the Patriarchal Narratives   97

betray various hallmarks of oral composition and which are verbatim transcriptions of speech. But these oral indicators are not nearly so discernible as had once been thought. This is not to say that those who seek to classify written texts should not use the terminology of oral genres. Rather we should not blur the distinctions which exist between oral and written narratives of the same genre. Obviously with a text such as the Bible we are (in the absence of indications to the contrary) dealing with the 'frozen record' of what may have been an oral performance given either as entertainment or for the purpose of recording historical events. But this possible oral context cannot and should not be assumed on the basis of genre distinctions. The exegete must provide clear evidence for the detection of an oral form behind a written text. Certainly there are means which can be used to judge whether or not a text originally had an oral existence, but this should not be determined on genre identification alone. To designate a specific written text as a legend, a fable, or any other tale type, because it shows similarities with oral genres, does not necessarily mean that the written text was originally oral, only that it may resemble oral forms.

3. *Genre Classification and History*

The issue of genre classification is intimately bound up with the question of historicity. The acceptance of the historical veracity of an event depends in large part on the classification of the genre of that literary form. Thus the distinctions which Gunkel and Gressmann made between legend and history writing were essential in establishing the qualitative difference between the literature recorded in Genesis and that found in the court history.

My intention is not to offer an analysis of the techniques and forms of what is referred to as 'history writing' in the ancient Near East.[122] I am interested only in establishing what is meant when we acknowledge a difference between history writing and creative story-telling. For Gunkel, historical reflection could only take place with the aid of writing. I have already maintained that this was a consequence of the romantic and/or linguistic theory of his time, which tended to argue for the priority of the spoken word over the written. Given this presupposition, history writing is seen as a later development of such oral genres as folktales and legends. Indeed, if T. Todorov is correct and genres are not created *ex nihilo* but emerge out of genres of the past,[123] then it would seem possible (as Gunkel argued) to write a history of literature tracing its development from simple forms to the more complex and sophisticated art of history writing. My concern, however, is the issue of orality. A discussion (albeit brief) of the concept of oral history, its composition and transmission is therefore essential.

In so far as folklorists have been interested in oral forms of tradition, oral history has not escaped their notice. Non-literate societies do communicate history and have, therefore, a concept of what constitutes the historical. How it is communicated and how we can judge the veracity of what is being communicated will now be discussed.

a. *Oral History and the Patriarchal Narratives*

The clear-cut distinctions between legend and history writing offered by both Gunkel and Gressmann are far more complicated than their writing would lead us to assume. Any suggestion of a simple continuity from legend to history writing can no longer be sustained. This has most recently been demonstrated by Van Seters.[124] His primary concern has been with the literary forms of history writing. My concern is with studies of oral forms of history narration, and what light they shed on whether or not the patriarchal narratives are written accounts or transcriptions of oral, tribal history.

Gunkel's attempt to differentiate between legend and historical writing has been referred to above (see p. 24) and was shown to be based on the conviction that Genesis would be better understood if the reported events were identified as legend and not as history. This was not to preclude the possibility that popular tradition in the form of legend could not contain historical memories. Rather, Gunkel argued that because of their originally oral form, traditions would become corrupted, and therefore legend was not a reliable source of history. Legend could be differentiated from history writing on the basis of the following criteria: Whereas legend was originally oral, history was always found in written form. The scope of history is concerned with events that affected the whole of the state, whereas legend chooses more intimate and personal details to recall. Thus history is concerned with the political, whereas legend is concerned with the familial. The historian is at pains to establish his connection with the eyewitness to the events he records. In the case of legend, however, it is not necessary to claim such a connection. The

3. Folklore Studies and the Patriarchal Narratives

repetition of tradition is enough. In the case of the patriarchal narratives, Gunkel suggests that the four hundred years in which the ancient Hebrews were in Egypt is too long a period for oral tradition to preserve an authentic record of past history.[125] Finally, history and legend speak of God in two different registers. In the former, since the scale of events is greater, the language used to speak of God is more impersonal, whereas in the case of the latter it is much more intimate and hence the author uses more anthropomorphic language, which itself emphasizes the fabulous and the incredible. Gunkel makes it clear, however, that this distinction between the fabulous and the anthropomorphic found within legend as opposed to history, is not a distinction which we as readers impose upon the text:

> The distinction between legend and history is not injected into the Old Testament, but is to be found by any attentive reader already present in the Old Testament.[126]

This would seem to imply that the author and his contemporary audience would have been well aware of the difference in genre.

The final and most important distinction to be made between history and legend is that the first is written in prose and the second, although not in form, is 'by nature poetry'.[127] By implication, therefore, given Gunkel's presupposition that poetry was the primary form of creative speech, legend should be considered as organic and existing from the very beginning of Hebrew life. Its purpose was 'to please, to elevate, to inspire and to move'.[128] For Gunkel it is only the barbarian who thinks that the true value of the narrative lies in its being treated as prose and therefore as history.[129]

According to Gunkel, then, not only were the narratives in Genesis to be understood as legend, but they were also composed with the understanding that they were not history and did not attempt to recount historical events. If they do contain historical memories it is only by chance that these have been preserved, for the 'legend has woven a poetic veil about the historical memories and hidden their outlines'.[130] Nonetheless, the legends are not to be thought of as 'free creation of the imagination' for they are anchored in data which comes from 'reflexion, tradition or observation'.[131] To say that the legend was not intended as history does not mean that it was bereft of all history, however. It is, not least, historically rooted. The stuff of legend is not merely imaginative construct but may also be the product of reflection upon historical events and/or people.

For Gunkel the events chronicled in Genesis are not historical memories preserved by story-tellers. Nonetheless, however long the period of time through which these stories passed, both at the oral and then at the written stage, there still remains within these legends certain elements which could only have pertained to an earlier period of history. By isolating these elements, a development from earlier to later periods may be detected, thereby making it possible to reconstruct a *Literaturgeschichte*:

> We cannot get a complete general view of the changes made by the collections... Thus the legends now make the impression of an old and originally many colored painting that has been many times retouched and has grown dark with age.[132]

Those responsible for collecting these legends, while altering the tales in accordance with their own bias, cannot be considered authors. Their main concern was to record the material with fidelity, a quality which Gunkel maintained was particularly apparent in Genesis.

These legends, although written down in the ninth and eighth centuries BCE, were originally much older and do therefore contain information of a more primitive history.[133] So, the tribal and race names preserved within the legends are forgotten in other records.[134] Accordingly, they must be considered as having belonged to prehistoric times. For example, if the legends of Genesis are compared with those of Judges, what is clear is that (with the exception of Judges 1), the legends of Judges no longer speak of tribes as persons:

> In the earlier portion of the period of Judges, then, this naive style of narrative disappeared so far as we can ascertain; from that time on such narratives are merely transmitted, but no longer constructed new.[135]

With regard to history therefore, whereas the legends of the book of Judges can be considered as historical, the ethnographic aspect of the Genesis legends cannot:

> We call these legends 'historical' when they reflect historical occurrences, 'ethnographic' when they contain chiefly descriptions of race and tribal relations. Thus we characterize the legend of the treaty of Beersheba and the various legends of migration as 'historical' but those of Jacob and Esau as 'ethnographic'.[136]

3. Folklore Studies and the Patriarchal Narratives

Gunkel's aesthetic appreciation of the legends contained within Genesis predominates in his analysis. Although the legends have had a long transmission history it is not because of the history they might contain that they are to be valued. Unlike others who have regarded the historical as the highest and indeed sometimes the only truth to be sought in biblical material, Gunkel makes an eloquent plea for an acceptance of poetic and not merely historical truth:

> And so although the things of the past are hidden rather than revealed in the legends, he would be a barbarian who would despise them on this account, for often they are more valuable than would be prosaic reports of actual occurrences.[137]

It is clear, then, that Gunkel did not consider the possibility of orally transmitted history. In accordance with his definition of legend, historical events are not recounted in ths form. Of course Gunkel's position, although shared by Gressmann and followed in large part by von Rad, was in total opposition to the view represented later by Albright and Bright, both of whom accepted the patriarchal narratives as reflecting a patriarchal period in pre-Israelite history.

The debate would not seem to have subsided. We are still left with the alternatives. Either the patriarchal narratives consist mainly of legendary material which is in large part ahistorical, if not fictitious, or they contain the history, however minimal, of what is designated as 'the patriarchal age'. The hope that archaeological finds would provide the needed evidence to support the dating of such a period in the second millennium has not been fulfilled and the data have been shown to be inconclusive.[138]

b. *Oral Traditions and Historical Reliability*

In 1972, R.C. Culley prsented a review of various studies undertaken in the field of oral history.[139] While recognizing that legends may contain a mixture of historical and non-historical material, Culley posed the question why scholars were always more interested in the historical elements of a story, rather than those features which make it interesting.[140]

Bearing this in mind, and not wanting to detract from the analysis of story as entertaiment, it is nonetheless necessary to ask what relationship exists between history and the genre category of legend. However entertaining the patriarchal stories may be, the reader cannot totally ignore their claim to be an accurate account of the lives of the founding families of the nation Israel.

In his book *De la tradition orale: essai de méthode historique*,[141] J. Vansina provided what was then the most systematic discussion to date on the value of oral traditions as historical sources. His book is the outcome of work carried out amongst pre-literate societies in the Congo, in Rwanda and Burundi, from 1953-1960. Vansina's primary contention is that oral tradition can and does contain valuable historical information.

Vansina's work contains a refutation of T.O. Beidelman, who had maintained that by the time oral traditions were written down they merely reflected the world view and particular perception of the time of writing.[142] Vansina is prepared to accept this premise only with reference to 'traditions of origins and migrations which may reflect cosmology more than history and may be entirely fictional'.[143] In general however, Vansina has stressed the need to demonstrate that a tradition is not historical, rather than placing the onus of proof upon those who wish to maintain that it is.

Regretting the lack of a typology of oral traditions, Vansina suggests a provisional classification in order to emphasize that each genre category has its own limitations, biases and means of representing the past. The aspect of the typology which relates to the patriarchal narratives is that which he designates as 'tale'. This category contains a sub-category of historical tales within which Vansina identifies three types: (1) tales which are concerned with general history; (2) tales which are concerned with local history; (3) tales which are concerned with family history. In the case of those tales concerned with general history, their provenance is mainly tribal. What is worth noting is Vansina's assertion that 'general history is only found in centralized societies',[144] and not in those tribal societies whose political structures depend upon kinship links. Because these traditions are always official they are the most likely to be distorted in defence of public interest. Tales concerned with local history are told of small units within a state, do not have a long historical memory, and are not transmitted with as much care as tales which are concerned with general history. The history which is recounted in these tales is normally that of the family, clan or village. The third group of tales, those which recount family history, are usually found in societies which have no centralized government, and replace general histories. This does not mean, however, that such family tales would disappear in societies which develop a centralized form of government. Indeed, very often these family tales

3. Folklore Studies and the Patriarchal Narratives 103

become the general history of a society because the 'family history in question is that of the dynasty'.[145] It is family histories which contain histories of migrations from neighbouring villages or localities. These may be useful as commentaries on genealogies, but they should be utilized with caution. They are also useful checks on historical migrations. However, because many of the recollections consist of unimportant details, they become similar to personal recollections, and can only be used in reconstructing the recent past.

In discussing the limitations of oral traditions Vansina compares the histories of states with those of segmentary societies. In the case of the former, history is fairly well transmitted and reaches far back in the past, whereas in segmentary societies the opposite is true.[146] The history of micro-societies, those whose largest social group is the extended family or families, will be careless in the manner in which they transmit traditions and will never extend far into the past. In short:

> Oral traditions are conditioned by the society in which they flourish... no oral tradition can transcend the boundaries of the social system in which it exists... the factor which most imparts bias and imposes limitations is the political system.[147]

Those oral traditions which are most susceptible to bias are traditions of creation, origin and migration. Vansina argues that traditions of 'genesis' cannot be taken literally as traditions of origin.[148]

Another interesting aspect of oral history is the manner in which it conveys time. The inability of oral history to establish, let alone maintain a correct assessment of the length of the past it is reporting is a well-documented phenomenon. Although the telescoping of events in the past sometimes occurs, more frequently what happens is that the time sequence of the past is lengthened.[149]

But at what stage does oral history become irretrievably confused and distorted by various biases? When does the historical become the fictional? Obviously no account of history can be called objective in the sense of being free from bias. Even the very choice of what is remembered reflects a bias and will affect the presentation of an event. Is there, however, a period of time after which oral history loses its ability to recount verifiable facts? For R.M. Dorson the period of time is 150 years.

> After a sufficient lapse of time, say a century and a half, all oral tradition becomes pure fiction.[150]

Certainly the results obtained by Duprée in his field work in Afghanistan would seem to substantiate such an assertion. Using the document reports of the British army as a control, Duprée followed the route which the British army took in the 1840s in an effort to record the stories from the period told by professional story-tellers of the community. These story-tellers were all illiterate, and most had been told the stories by the previous generation. Duprée's results clearly demonstrate the way oral tradition acquires folktale motifs and fabulous aspects while still maintaining a certain core of documented evidence from the period.[151] Given that the core had been reduced considerably over the decades one wonders how long it will be before the entire account of the events becomes fictional. Nonetheless, Dorson's period of 150 years does seem somewhat arbitrary. For example, in his preface J. Vansina maintains that in the African states he is dealing with, no oral history is obtainable for any time before 1700.[152] On the other hand, J.C. Miller has documented evidence showing the veracity of oral history amongst the Imbangala in Angola, who in some cases preserve over a period of three hundred years: 'a nucleus of historical fact even while the historians who recite the episode surround it with fictional artistic elaborations'.[153]

Perhaps the most significant point Miller makes about these oral histories is their synchronic, timeless quality. This quality is conveyed by the Imbangala's insistence upon viewing the past as a reflection of their contemporary social and political structures:

> Imbangala historians... view past centuries through the prism of social and political conditions of their own time, seeking the origins of descent groups, political titles and structural relationships which have importance in the present.[154]

Miller's use of oral traditions to reconstruct Angolan history prior to the Portuguese, however, is only justified because there is so much written documentation with which to compare the oral accounts and thereby to act as a control.[155]

Miller's study of oral history recounting in Angola provides an interesting modern parallel to the oral history debate in Old Testament studies. The use of oral history in reconstructing historical events has never received unqualified acceptance by the majority of historians. Although Vansina argued for the dependability of oral traditions and attempted to restore confidence in the use of such sources, subsequent field studies have not substantiated many

3. Folklore Studies and the Patriarchal Narratives   105

of his claims for the veracity of oral history.[156] In fact, in his latest study of oral history amongst the Kuba of Zaire, he has had to qualify many of his previous conclusions, stating that the historian must be even more cautious in his use of oral traditions than had previously been suggested.[157]

From his work with the Imbangala of modern-day Angola, J.C. Miller has been cautious in his use of oral traditions. Nonetheless, he has attempted to legitimate a method of using oral accounts to fill in the gaps in the wrtten documents of the missionaries of the late seventeenth century. The particular sources for his reconstruction are taken from the accounts rendered in the *Malunda*. This is the name given to the narratives which the Imbangala use to recount their history. This category of narrative is only a sub-category of a much broader group of tales, which are non-historical but which share a similar structure. For the Imbangala, these *Malunda* are recounted in connection with the names recited in genealogies known as *Musendo*. Having recited a genealogy, the oral historian will recount a number of standardized narrative episodes, *Malunda*, in connection with each name in the genealogy. The historian will draw on similar narratives in order to make the same point about different titles and descent groups. These of course can be altered and embellished, depending upon the artistic skills of the historian.[158] 'Nonetheless, whatever the flexibility of detail, there remains a stable central point of each episode, which has in some cases remained stable for decades.'[159]

The Imbangala are highly selective as to which aspects of the past they preserve, tending to retain only those which have present-day analogies.[160] Furthermore, they tend only to preserve historical data which 'establish social or political precedent influencing contemporary behaviour patterns'.[161] It is largely as a result of the Imbangala regarding their history as concerned with the present, that their particular presentations of the ancient past acquire a synchronic timelessness—a characteristic more frequently associated with the folktale.

Although some oral historians are capable of stringing together a number of *Malunda* to give the impression of historical chronology, the episodic order is of their own creation. Each *Malunda* can be recounted separately. It has its own internal unity and does not depend on other episodes for its meaning. The possible plot which a skilful raconteur might deliver is not necessarily historically accurate. In this regard:

the Western historian would be ill-advised to mistake the plot line constructed by the performer for evidence of consistent historical development running through the entire story of narrative episodes ... the historical content of each episode must derive from its own internal logic. Clearly there can be no chronology, even relative, based on the order in which episodes may be told.[162]

Of course in this instance Miller can verify the accounts of the *Malunda* with written record to see how accurate a reflection of the past they present. There are many other case studies for which such a control does not exist.

Miller has argued that in general the *Malunda* display certain common characteristics:

1. They are self-contained narrative episodes, whose meaning is gained from an internal logic.
2. These narrative episodes are fairly standardized. Hence the same *Malunda* can be used of different people or events.
3. There exists, nonetheless, a certain amount of flexibility and variability in the way the *Malunda* are recounted.
4. Since each episode is independent of the others, it is the skill of the historian which unites the episodes into a longer integrated historical composition.
5. The past is preserved only when it is seen to have direct bearing on, or manifestation in, the present. The past is preserved to justify new lineage groups and property rights.

If a comparison were made between these elements and the distinctions made by H. Gunkel between legend and history writing, it is immediately evident that clear-cut genre distinctions do not exist. The *Malunda* are oral history. The scope of the stories, whilst affecting the state, nonetheless recall personal details, and are therefore as much concerned with political matters as they are with familial ones. The one other aspect which this oral history has in common with Gunkel's definition of legend is that both are short, self-contained units.

If the distinction between legend and historical writing is not one of form, and if both categories can have the same content and represent equivalent concerns, is the only valid distinction that of intention? If legend can be used to convey historical events, and historical events can contain legendary material, how are the two to be differentiated?

3. Folklore Studies and the Patriarchal Narratives

What recent folklore studies have demonstrated is that frequently historical narrative cannot be classified as a literary genre, distinguishable from other genre categories whether oral or written. Consequently the oral narratives which are sometimes designated as 'historical' narrative, can rarely be used as accurate sources. Speaking of African societies not affected by a written Arabic culture, R. Finnegan states:

> The common picture of formalized historical accounts being passed down from generation to generation by specialists whose duty it is to recite and transmit them accurately turns out to be not so widely applicable as one might think.[163]

That those who recount the narratives are convinced of their historical accuracy is in itself no absolute proof, especially since frequently the account reflects the interests of the official political and/or religious authorities.

The use of genealogies in reconstructing the social history of an area must also be questioned. Like the more formal narrative genres genealogies are also influenced by socio-political circumstances, and are modified accordingly. Unlike J. Vansina's assertion that the genealogical variants are due to lapses of memory,[164] Finnegan regards such changes as resulting from changed circumstances:

> Their (genealogies) actual use is always tied to some practical issue: there is never recitation or learning of genealogies as a whole for their own sake. Genealogies are thus used to fit particular facts, and are constantly being modified in the light of the current situation.[165]

In a more recent study, and to date the most comprehensive analysis of the nature and function of genealogies, R.R. Wilson has argued that oral genealogies do not 'function primarily as historical records'.[166] This is due largely to the fact that they reflect existing socio-political structures and not those of the past. The historical accuracy of any oral genealogy must remain suspect, therefore. Like oral historical narratives, oral genealogies are constantly reshaped and modified to reflect the present concerns of the community. In his work in the Gambia, D.R. Wright has shown just how drastic these changes can be and records an instance of a clan altering their traditions of origin for political reasons.[167] The main purpose behind Wright's research is to provide empirical evidence for the rapidity with which oral history narratives change, are embellished, and finally reconstituted. Whereas one might expect non-historical tales to alter in the telling, or utilize stock scenes or phrases, what is essential in this instance is that these story-tellers are convinced, or at least maintain to their listeners, that no change in the narration has taken place. As P. Irwin reminds us, 'Tradition does not merely transmit the past: it creates it'.[168] From Wright's field work it would seem that where a society transmits its historical recollections orally, the extent to which they are transformed in the light of the present raises severe problems for the retrieval of any historically accurate detail. In his latest work Vansina has moved so far from his previous confidence in the historical veracity of oral tradition as to state in respect of Kuba oral history:

> The main process of building oral history involves not so much a passive, haphazard loss of memory as an active choice of items to remember, and that choice is dictated by their perception of history ... whether that community is a clan section, a village, a chiefdom, or the kingdom.[169]

But this is not a new assertion. Certainly Wellhausen maintained the improbability of retrieving historical facts from the patriarchal narratives, and whereas Gunkel considered the possibility that the narratives did contain elements retained from different historical periods, he nonetheless realized that these legends should not be taken as historical record.

Nevertheless, the idea that oral history can maintain factual accuracy over extended periods of time, still persists.[170] Even where scholars express doubts as to the reliability of the patriarchal narratives, they not infrequently suggest a sociological setting for these narratives. Thus it is argued that even if the events told in the stories are not historically accurate, their setting nevertheless reflects an accurate picture of the pre-settlement period of Israelite history. Theirs is a portrayal of a nomadic life-style which actually obtained prior to the exodus. The stories, therefore, although not the result of an accurate reconstruction of that way of life, handed down by word of mouth throughout the centuries.

As we have seen, however, this ignores the fact that the process of oral transmission inevitably involves a reconstruction of the very past it seeks to preserve.

As I hope this brief survey has shown, cultures which convey the past via oral prose narrative reconstruct their past in accordance

3. Folklore Studies and the Patriarchal Narratives

with changing social circumstances.[171] What will be remembered of the past, is that which is important for the present. As J. Vansina has concluded:

> Communications presupposes society and all messages are social products. Hence messages of oral tradition have a 'social surface'. They are significant to members of the communities in which they are told. Otherwise they would not be communicated at all. Would the social pressures not alter the contents of a message? No doubt this occurs, and, as all messages from tradition are uttered in the present, when they are recorded they are strongly influenced by the social present.[172]

What is also clear is that there is no simple technique for establishing the length of time it takes for legendary material to obscure the historical event itself. In some instances it is a relatively short period of time (i.e. one generation) and in others as long as 150 years.

If Westermann's analysis of the legends in Genesis is accepted and the 'family saga' is the earliest form of oral tradition, having a long prehistory before the formation of the state,[173] then Vansina's warnings against using such traditions to establish the events of history should be taken seriously:

> The history of micro-societies—that is, societies in which there is no social group larger than the extended families (a camp)—is pretty well non-existent. Traditions are carelessly transmitted, do not go far back and are always of a folk nature.[174]

As for the idea that family concerns as reflected in 'family sagas' are the oldest oral genre, and that wherever such concerns are recorded we have the oldest form of the tradition, this too is not proven. Very often a family history will become the general history of that society. When this happens it usually vindicates the position of the present rulers and will inevitably be biased in their favour. The circumstances which such histories recount are therefore not necessarily more ancient or historical. Nor is there automatically a simple progression from family history to general state history. The genre 'family saga' tells us nothing of its historical age, nor anything about the historical veracity of the sociological setting it portrays. There is no modern evidence to suggest that oral family history predates general state histories or that the rate of change in transmission is any less than any other oral genre.

The problems of drawing analogies between the patriarchal narratives and the Icelandic family sagas have been discussed above[175] and shown to be highly tenuous, if not totally erroneous. Not least the primary orality of both is still questionable. The nearest equivalent genre in oral history to that of the patriarchal stories is those family lineages, which in turn come to represent the general history of the state. This does not, however, mean that such histories arose in response to the actual events they record. In so far as they become the means of state legitimation they cease to be reliable sources of the events of the remote past. Furthermore, recent studies have shown that oral histories rarely retain an accurate record of the length of the past they recount. As D.P. Henige has demonstrated in his work with the Fante and Ashante and their oral history,

> One's view of the past, including its duration, is more the product of the exigencies of the present than of the dispassionate desire to portray past events as they actually occurred.[176]

His final conclusion is that no accurate chronological evidence of past events can be found in oral history for periods prior to that history's actual transcription.[177]

c. *Conclusions*
The overwhelming weight of evidence which suggests that oral histories behave in the same way as other oral genres cannot be overlooked. Nor is it possible to establish clear-cut distinctions between the historical interests of non-literate and literate societies. Primary oral societies would seem to have the same interests in past events as do literate societies, and the history they tell appears to have the same function. Likewise the form in which such histories are told does not differ radically.

Of course the most striking difference between oral and written history is the effect it produces. Obviously, a written text is more difficult to alter, modify and change than its oral equivalent. It preserves once and for all a particular argument or point of view. A written text can be compared with other accounts of the same event, in a way which an oral account precludes.

This brief discussion of oral history has been necessary in order to indicate that the narrative forms it uses are frequently indistinguishable from other genres. Fiction and fact, these two distinct categories of thought frequently share the same form, that of narrative. That the events of the historical narrative are believed to be true by both the performer and the audience, is too subjective a criterion on which

3. Folklore Studies and the Patriarchal Narratives 111

to base the veracity of the account. Whereas with written records the historian can analyse, and on the basis of subsequent information evaluate the evidence recorded, by definition with oral history this is impossible. For such a history is in its transmission in a constant state of transformation. In his commentary on Genesis, G.W. Coats has maintained that history differs from saga and legend in that:

> History writing marks a movement away from the context of the family or tribe with their story telling concerns, to the record keeping responsibilities of the nation... It derives from the concern to document the past of the people in order to validate the present administration.[178]

Yet it is precisely this story-telling technique which is used by oral societies to recount their history. It is not always the case that such story-telling takes place only within the context of the family or tribe, not least because these stories can become part of the general history of a society with a centralized government. Just as written records seek to legitimize the present ruling political or religious authorities, so too do oral accounts. Distinctions between what have been considered as older oral genres and history writing cannot therefore be made. History writing inevitably includes written forms of oral genres such as legend and folktale. It does not necessarily reflect a more sophisticated and complex way of viewing the world. Oral histories can equally be as complex and sophisticated in the way they seek to manipulate the events of the past.

Oral societies have a need to chronicle their past. That they do so is now a matter of record. Unlike the written document however, oral history has no means of verifying the events it seeks to record. Therefore, the rate of a history's transformation in the process of oral transmission is too great to allow for an accurate record of historical events over extended periods of time. This must be borne in mind whenever the patriarchal narratives are used to reconstruct a presettlement period.

As for distinguishing a specific oral history genre from other oral genres, the necessary criteria are difficult to list, probably because they do not exist. The degree to which a historical event is obscured by the elaboration of the performer is variable. What has been shown, however, is that such elaboration and modification takes place on a larger scale and at a quicker rate than has previously been thought. Appeals to the sacred nature of the history contained in the biblical text cannot be ignored, since this has often been seen to be the conservative influence affecting the rate of change of a text even at the oral stage.[179] Yet here, too, the evidence from other oral societies does not confirm this opinion. Where there exists a structured form of religious practice and established religious institutions then one might suspect that oral transmission of a religious tradition would be less likely to allow for radical transformation. Yet mention of such institutions is not made during the pre-Mosaic period. The likelihood that any tribal history, sacred or otherwise, could have been preserved at the oral stage for a period longer than two hundred years before being committed to writing cannot be substantiated on the basis of any recent fieldwork in anthropology or folklore. If the patriarchal narratives were at one time tribal history originating during the pre-Mosaic period, then what we have now can only be considered as folktale. Even if this tribal history was composed during the time of settlement and written down some two hundred years later, the extent to which it can testify to historical events is negligible.

4. General Conclusions

This chapter has explored some of the issues and problems involved in genre classification. Gunkel and others following him appealed to folktale motifs, which the biblical text had in common with primitive oral tales of other cultures, in order to uphold the antiquity of the patriarchal narratives. We have seen, however, that such folktale motifs are no proof of a text's orality, let alone its antiquity. Recent research by Zipes and Ellis on the work of the brothers Grimm, for example, has shown that part of their 'editorial' activity consisted in the introduction of many of these motifs. Far from being a verbatim transcription of oral tales, their collection was in fact a highly literate creation, owing so much to its editors that it cannot be used as evidence of the oral compositions which lie behind the work. Furthermore, given that the tales in the Grimms' collection were themselves the products of highly literate and educated sources familiar with the writings of other cultures—including those of the ancient Near East—it is hardly surprising that they would in all probability echo motifs found in biblical narratives. These common motifs, therefore, are not necessarily independent of each other. Similarly, the Thompson tale motif index only tells us that a particular tale motif existed in the ancient Near East, and indicates how all-pervasive Judaeo-Christian influence has been upon subsequent folktales. It does not necessarily furnish evidence that any particular motif is confined to, or is typical of, oral genres.

The folklore categories of folktale, legend, myth and their subcategories are by definition oral. This does not mean, however, that they do not exist in written form, and when we refer to their presence in the biblical text it is important that they should be distinguished from one another. Yet these genre classifications are not confined to oral narratives. Neither can we list them in a chronological order whereby one genre inevitably pre-dates another. In fact there can be no certainty in claims that form is an indicator of age. So, for example, an appeal to the brevity of composition as a sure sign of its antiquity, is immediately contradicted in the example of Jacob by the fact that the folktale (a complex and multi-episodic form) was considered by Gunkel to have been the original 'kernel' of the Jacob legends in Genesis.

Finally, it has been argued that historiography is not only confined to literate societies. Non-literate communities also have historiographies not infrequently utilizing the same genre as those of written history. The essential difference between oral and written historiography is that change is more extensive and rapid in oral histories, sacred or otherwise. This fact will have repercussions for our view of the patriarchal narratives. If they are thought of as oral tribal histories, then appeal to their historical veracity can only be made if the period between the origin of the stories and their written transmission was a relatively short one. That the patriarchal narratives purport to recount the history of various ancestral characters and their encounters with God is clear. But are these literary fictions or historical figures? Does the genre of the patriarchal narratives itself designate the difference between literary fiction and historiography? If, as has been argued, distinctions between the narrative genres of myth, legend and folktale are dependent upon the perceptions of each particular culture, the indicators given in each performance, and the expectations of the listeners, then classification becomes difficult for any who are not part of the original audience. Contemporary judgments of biblical narrative genres are, therefore, largely subjective.

When considering how oral societies communicate history, the most that can be said is that they do not keep accurate records of events over extended periods of time (i.e. more than 150 years). If these narratives are, therefore, an attempt to record the events of a pre-Mosaic period, they cannot be considered as historically accurate, unless, that is, Moses was the author. These narratives like any others will inevitably reflect the period in which they are written. If they had a separate oral history then the historical reminiscences of an earlier period will have been altered in transmission.

If we accept the possibility that the earliest date for these written patriarchal narratives was during the Davidic/Solomonic period, then the only possible history they could substantiate would be the 150 years prior to their being written.

Chapter 4

CONCLUSIONS

It has been the contention of this work that many of the conclusions of earlier biblical scholars with regard to oral composition and transmission can no longer be sustained. Too often their presuppositions were based on previous findings of folklore studies which today would be repudiated. Whereas former generations considered that they had established the means for uncovering the original oral form of a received written text, now these criteria are seen as insufficient and in some cases incorrect. Furthermore, the various tale collections which have been so painstakingly amassed from all over the world, while providing insights into oral compositions and their transmission, have produced very few results which would help determine their relative age. So the antiquity of folklore forms, once generally agreed upon, is no longer held with the same conviction and assurance of earlier generations of folklorists. Certainly, the outcome of research into oral history (both in its composition and transmission) can no longer provide biblical scholars with the same degree of confidence in either its antiquity or historical veracity.

Previously biblical scholars have had recourse to the results achieved in the study of folklore, and by analogy have used these to substantiate at least some of their claims for the pre-history of ancient Israel. In the forms of oral tales from other societies they have seen genres analogous to the written texts of the Old Testament. In the case of the patriarchal narratives they have isolated those written forms which, it was argued, had had an extended period of oral existence prior to their transcription.

This assumption of orality led scholars such as Gunkel to maintain that oral genres (such as the legend) were not the vehicle of historical reminiscences, since these were unique to written genres. Written and oral genres could be distinguished from one another by oth form and content. The oral forms which were the original precursors of the written text had been created for the purpose of entertainment. Other scholars, whilst agreeing with Gunkel that the legend was not primarily concerned with recounting historical events, nonetheless thought that it preserved certain tribal memories which had been transmitted in some instances prior to the occupation of the land. In spite of their differences both positions presume a lengthy oral transmission history for the material. Whether historicized fiction or fictionalized history, these legends were presumed to have originated in a period which long antedated the beginning of the monarchy.

Relying on this presumption of orality, many of the narrative duplications were seen as evidence of original oral composition and/or transmission variants behind the written versions. It has been shown, however, that distinguishing between oral and written texts on the basis of certain stylistic features is no longer tenable. This essay has also demonstrated that another supposed indicator of orality, the presence of 'tale motifs', cannot be used to determine the original orality of a received written text. Tale motifs are not necessarily confined to oral genres, and therefore the comparison of biblical motifs with those common to oral societies cannot provide any assurance as to the text's oral origin.

Furthermore, genre classifications are also now seen to be no guide to a narrative's oral or written character. Neither do they provide evidence of a composition's relative age, since the presence of a particular genre is no indication of a work's antiquity. Therefore to classify the patriarchal narratives as legend is not thereby to presume either their oral or ancient origins.

Modern folklorists with their emphasis upon studying each oral presentation of a tale as a unique performance have shifted the focus of scholarly attention away from the search for the original form of the oral narrative. Each performance is in a sense the original, and therefore it is meaningless to speak of an *Urtext*.

An appreciation of this element of re-creation as integral to composition has necessitated a change in our perception of the process of oral transmission. Therefore the notion of a faithful transmission of an oral composition, whether as entertainment or historical reminiscence, of a profane or sacred text, is now seen to be far less of a phenomenon of oral societies than had previously been supposed. Until the early 1960s it was widely held that oral societies

4. Conclusions

had a greater capacity for retaining accurate accounts of oral compositions than more book-bound cultures. With the work of Parry and Lord, however, memorization is no longer seen as the key to a culture's oral narrative transmission. We now know that it is not necessarily the case that story-tellers in oral societies memorize their tales. Instead it is now appreciated that they are capable of retaining fairly lengthy oral compositions aided by epithets, formulaic phrases and patterns. Each performance of the same composition contains both stable and creative elements, however. The most recent folklore research has shown, furthermore, that even the presence of epithets or formulaic phrases in a written text is no sure touchstone of its orality. Like repetition these features can also be part of written techniques.

For our understanding of the patriarchal narratives, one of the more significant findings of modern folklore is that oral compositions are rarely preserved unchanged over an extended period of time. Although few in number, those studies which have followed the careers of story-tellers over several decades have demonstrated the considerable change which is involved in each retelling of the stories. This suggests that oral tradition, far from preserving the sources of its past (whether they be entertainment or historical recollection, or both) constantly reinterprets that past in the light of the present. Indeed, one of the hallmarks of tradition is not that it conserves the past but rather that it is constantly evolving in such a way as to incorporate the changes of different historical periods and circumstances. The written transcription of presumed oral tales will inform us more, therefore, about the period in which those tales were transcribed than about the period in which they were presumed to have been composed.

It is therefore evident that the 'assured results' of form criticism concerning oral composition and transmission can no longer be accepted with reference either to the origins or the antiquity of the patriarchal narratives.

NOTES

Notes to Chapter 1

1. J.G. Frazer, *Folk-lore in the Old Testament*, 2 vols. (London, 1918).
2. Cf. S. Thompson, *The Folktale* (London, 1946), pp. 382-85, for a discussion of Frazer's methodology; for a discussion of W. Robertson-Smith's influence on Frazer, cf. T.O. Beidelman, *W. Robertson-Smith and the Sociological Study of Religion* (London, 1974), pp. 49-61.
3. Frazer, *op. cit.*, I, p. vii.
4. For a critique of his position, see S. Thompson, *The Folktale* (London, 1977), pp. 382-85.
5. Frazer, *op. cit.*, II, p. 371, 'The historian who attributes the observance of them (i.e. the customs) to Jacob and good authority for doing so, whether he describes the customs from personal observation or merely from oral tradition'.
6. *Ibid.*, II, p. 371.
7. For a discussion of this see pp. 101-10.
8. Frazer, *op. cit.*, II, p. 39.
9. *Ibid.*, II, p. 371.
10. J. Wellhausen's dismissal of the possibility of gaining any historical insights from oral tradition may be seen as an acceptance of a degeneration theory. See p. 22.
11. F.L. Utley, 'Folk Literature: An Operational Definition', in *The Study of Folklore*, ed. A. Dundes (Englewood Cliffs, 1965), pp. 7-24.
12. W. Thoms, 'Folklore' in *The Study of Folklore*, ed. A. Dundes (Englewood Cliffs, 1965), pp. 4-6.
13. *Funk and Wagnalls Standard Dictionary of Folklore Mythology and Legend*, ed. M. Leach (London, 1972), pp. 398-402.
14. W.R. Bascom, 'Verbal Art', *JAF* 68 (1955), pp. 245-52; Maranda K.E., 'The Concept of Folklore', *Midwest Folklore* 13 (1963), p. 85.
15. D. Ben-Amos, 'Toward a Definition of Folklore in Context', *Toward New Perspectives in Folklore*, ed. A. Parades and R. Bauman (Austin, 1972), p. 8.
16. S. Thompson, 'Folklore at Midcentury', *Midwest Folklore* 1 (1951), p. 11.
17. F. Utley, *op. cit.*, p. 8.
18. D. Ben-Amos, *op. cit.*, p. 13.
19. J.W. Rogerson, *Anthropology and the Old Testament* (Oxford, 1978),

p. 66.
20. *Ibid.*, p. 66.
21. D. Ben-Amos, *op. cit.*, p. 131.
22. *Ibid.*, p. 14.
23. R.M. Dorson, *Folklore and Fakelore* (London, 1976), p. 33.
24. L. Dégh and A. Vazsonyi, 'The Memorate and the Proto Memorate', *JAF* 87 (1974), p. 238.
25. W. Klatt, *Hermann Gunkel* (FRLANT 100; Göttingen, 1969), esp. pp. 129-44; P. Gibert, *Une Théorie de la légende* (Paris, 1979), esp. pp. 43-55, 123. 'Gunkel profite aussi ... du folklorisme de son temps. Entrant dans le jeu d'un certain vocabulaire, il entre aussi dans le jeu d'une certaine vision populaire. Et c'est avec cette vision typique qu'il aborde encore la Genèse' (p. 202).
26. B.M. Warner, 'Primitive Saga Men', *VT* 29 (1979), pp. 325-35.
27. J. Wellhausen, 'Die Composition des Hexateuchs', *Jahrbücher für Deutsche Theologie* XXI (1876), pp. 392-450, 531-602; XXII (1877), pp. 407-79.
28. J. Wellhausen, *Geschichte Israels* I (Berlin, 1878) republished as *Prolegomena zur Geschichte Israels* (Berlin, 1883). All references to the *Prolegomena zur Geschichte Israels* are to the third edition (Berlin, 1886). The ET is taken from J. Wellhausen, *Prolegomena to the History of Israel* (Edinburgh, 1885) from 2nd edn, 1883.
29. *Ibid.*, ET p. 366 (German pp. 382f.)
30. *Ibid.*, ET p. 23 (German p. 23).
31. *Ibid.*, ET pp. 404-10 (German pp. 420-28).
32. *Ibid.*, ET p. 345 (German p. 360).
33. *Ibid.*, ET p. 321 (German p. 335).
34. Succeeding generations of literary critics, however, have attempted to modify the four document scheme together with the relative datings given to their sources. So R. Smend, in *Die Erzählung des Hexateuch auf ihre Quellen untersucht* (Berlin, 1912), considered the Yahwistic corpus to be the product of two separate sources which he denoted by the sigla J^1 and J^2, J^1 being the older of the two. O. Eissfeldt, in his *Hexateuch-Synopse* (Leipzig, 1922), accepted such a distinction but preferred to use the siglum L (lay Source) instead of J^1. Or again R.H. Pfeiffer, 'A Non-Israelite Source of the Book of Genesis', *ZAW* 48 (1930), pp. 66-73, detected a fifth source which he considered came from tenth-century Seir and thus designated it 'S'. C.A. Simpson accepted the two sources of Smend, but considered J^2 to be an elaboration of J^1 and not a parallel source in his *The Early Traditions of Israel: A Critical Analysis of the Pre-Deuteronomic Narrative of the Hexateuch* (London, 1950). Until recently and with the exception of certain Scandinavian scholars (cf. my thesis, pp. 63-73) the four document scheme has remained the working hypothesis for all biblical research.
35. *Op. cit.*, ET pp. 318-19 (German p. 331).

36. *Ibid.*, ET p. 339 (German p. 339).
37. *Ibid.*, ET p. 296 (German p. 309).
38. *Ibid.*, ET pp. 335-37 (German pp. 349-51).
39. *Contra* G.H. Ewald, *A History of Israel* (ET London, 1869 from the German 2nd edn, 1843), I, p. 25.
40. J. Wellhausen, *op. cit.*, ET p. 335 (German p. 351)
41. *Ibid.*, ET p. 327 (German p. 340).
42. *Ibid.*, ET p. 361 (German p. 377).
43. *Ibid.*, ET p. 294 (German p. 309).
44. *Ibid.*, ET p. 294 (German p. 309).
45. *Ibid.*, ET p. 333 (German p. 349).
46. *Ibid.*, ET p. 358 (German p. 376).
47. *Ibid.*, ET p. 312 (German p. 334).
48. *Ibid.*, ET p. 294 (German p. 309).
49. See D.A. Knight, 'Wellhausen and the Interpretation of Israel's Literature', *Semeia* 25 (1982), pp. 30-31.
50. Wellhausen *op. cit.*, ET p. 324 (German p. 339).
51. This is not to suggest that the interest shown by H. Gunkel and others in the oral precursor to the written text implied the rejection of the literary-critical conclusions of J. Wellhausen. Cf. D.A. Knight's comments in *Rediscovering the Traditions of Israel* (Missoula, 1974), pp. 72-80.
52. G. Ortutay, 'Jacob Grimm and Folklore Study in Hungary', *Hungarian Folklore* (1957), pp. 183-202.
53. J.L.C. and W.C. Grimm, *Kinder- und Hausmärchen* (Leipzig, 1812-1815), ET of 3rd German edn 1856, *Grimm's Household Tales* (London, 1892).
54. J.L.C. Grimm, *Deutsche Mythologie* (Göttingen, 1835).
55. Cf. R.M. Dorson, 'The Eclipse of Solar Mythology', *The Study of Folklore*, ed. A. Dundes (New Jersey, 1965), pp. 57-83. It is of interest that whereas the school of solar mythologists ceased to exist in England after Müller's death in 1900, a society of comparative mythology, upholding the self-same theories of solar mythology, was established in Berlin in 1906. See Dorson, *op. cit.*, p. 83; for a discussion of theories of comparative mythology and their influence on OT interpretation see J.W. Rogerson, *Myth in Old Testament Interpretation* (BZAW 134; Berlin, 1974), pp. 33-56.
56. A. Lang, Introduction to *Grimm's Household Tales*, pp. i-lxix. This was in agreement with J.L.C. Grimm, as can be seen in *Deutsche Mythologie*, I, pp. i-xxxiv.
57. *Grimm's Household Tales* (ET London, 1892).
58. H. Gunkel, *Schöpfung und Chaos in Urzeit und Endzeit* (Göttingen, 1895), p. 1.
59. *Ibid.*, p. 143. The translation of the German term *Sage* is a complex issue, not least because genre definitions have never been agreed within a particular discipline, let alone across disciplines. Because of the influence

folklore studies had exercised over form-critical categories in Old Testament studies, I have chosen to follow the practice of folklorists in their translation of the German term. For a fuller discussion see pp. 75-76.

60. Cf. H. Gunkel, *Genesis* (Göttingen, 1901). ET of 'Introduction', *The Legends of Genesis* (New York, 1964).

61. *Ibid.*, ET pp. 10-13 (German 3rd edn [1910] pp. viii-ix).

62. *Ibid.*, ET pp. 25-35 (German pp. xx-xxv).

63. *Ibid.*, ET p. 38 (German p. xviii).

64. *Ibid.*, ET pp. 38ff (German pp. xxix-xxx).

65. A. Olrik, 'Epische Gesetze der Volksdichtung', *Zeitschrift für Deutsches Altertum und Deutsche Literatur*, 51 (1909), pp. 1-12, ET *The Study of Folklore*, ed. A. Dundes (Englewood Cliffs, 1965), pp. 129-41. The reader need only consult the footnotes of Gunkel's 1910 commentary on Genesis, pp. xxxvii-lv, to see the extent of his reliance on Olrik.

66. But note B.M. Warner in his article, 'Primitive Saga Men', *VT* 29 (1979), pp. 325-35 who states that Olrik's theses 'could not have had much influence as they completely contradict Gunkel's theories of oral transmission' (p. 331). The above comparison refutes this judgment. For further reference see J.H. Hayes, *An Introduction to Old Testament Study* (Nashville, 1979), pp. 132ff.

67. The German term *Sage* is here retained to keep the sense in which Olrik used it, i.e. to refer to oral genres in general.

68. Gunkel, *Legends*, p. 42; *Genesis*, p. xxxii; *op. cit.*, ET p. 131 (German p. 2). Cf. A. Olrik.

69. Gunkel, *ibid.*, ET p. 83 (German p. liii). Cf. Olrik, *op. cit.*, pp. 132f. (German p. 3).

70. Gunkel *ibid.*, ET p. 49 (German p. xxxix). Cf. Olrik *op. cit.*, p. 133 (German p. 3). N.B. Olrik restricted the number to three. This did not mean to imply that other numbers could not exist, only that where they did they expressed a 'totally abstract quantity'.

71. Gunkel, *ibid.*, ET pp. 49f. (German p. xxxv). Cf. Olrik, who limits the number to two, *op. cit.*, ET p. 134 (German p. 5).

72. Gunkel, *ibid.*, ET pp. 44-69 (German p. xxxii and p. 69). Cf. Olrik, *op. cit.*, ET p. 137 (German p. 8).

73. Gunkel, *ibid.*, ET p. 45 (German p. xxxii). Cf. Olrik, *op. cit.*, ET p. 137 (German pp. 8f.).

74. Gunkel *ibid.*, ET p. 48 (German p. xxiv). Cf. Olrik *op. cit.*, ET p. 137 (German p. 9).

75. Gunkel *ibid.*, ET p. 53 (German p. xxxvi).

76. Gunkel, *ibid.*, ET p. 41 (German p. xxxi).

77. H. Gressmann, 'Sage und Geschichte in den Patriarchenerzählungen', *ZAW* 30 (1910), pp. 1-39.

78. W. Wundt, *Völkerpsychologie*, III/3 (Leipzig, 1909). See W. Klatt, *op. cit.*, pp. 134-36.

Notes to Chapter 1 123

79. H. Gunkel, *Genesis* p. lxi.
80. *Ibid.*, pp. lxxviff.
81. *Ibid.*, p. xxvi.
82. *Ibid.*, p. lix.
83. H. Gunkel, *Das Märchen im Alten Testament* (Tübingen, 1917), ET, *The Folktale in the Old Testament* (Sheffield, 1987).
84. R. Finnegan, *Oral Poetry* (Cambridge, 1977), p. 34.
85. J.G. Frazer, *Folk-lore in the Old Testament*, I (London, 1918), p. vii.
86. Finnegan, *op. cit.*, p. 37.
87. *Ibid.*, p. 39.
88. H. Gunkel, *Legends*, p. 40 (German p. xxx).
89. *Ibid.*, ET p. 54 (German p. xxxviii).
90. *Ibid.*, ET p. 40 (German p. xxx).
91. *Ibid.*, ET p. 41 (German p. xxxi).
92. *Ibid.*, ET p. 40 (German p. xxx).
93. *Ibid.*, ET p. 62 (German p. xli).
94. *Ibid.*, ET p. 47 (German p. xxxiv).
95. *Ibid.*, ET pp. 82-87 (German pp. xxxii and lii-lv) where Gunkel argues that the discursive style of the Joseph story betrays its later composition. He asserts that its style is so much more detailed that it should be classified as a short story (*Novelle*) rather than a legend. The *Novelle* style dates from the early period of the monarchy.
96. *Ibid.*, ET p. 45 (German p. xxxii).
97. *Ibid.*, ET p. 81 (German p. lii).
98. *Ibid.*, ET p. 81 (German p. lii).
99. *Ibid.*, ET p. 80 (German p. lii).
100. *Ibid.*, ET p. 96 (German p. lxiii).
101. *Ibid.*, ET p. 97 (German p. lxiv).
102. *Ibid.*, ET p. 98 (German p. lxiv).
103. *Ibid.* (German p. lxv).
104. *Ibid.*, ET pp. 98f. (German p. lxv).
105. *Ibid.*, ET p. 99 (German p. lxvi).
106. *Ibid.*, ET p. 101 (German pp. lxvi, lxvii).
107. *Ibid.*, ET p. 103 (German p. lxvii).
108. *Ibid.*, ET pp. 103-13 (German pp. lxvii-lxxii).
109. *Ibid.*, ET p. 138 (German pp. lxxxviiif.).
110. *Ibid.*, ET p. 123 (German pp. lxxvf.).
111. *Ibid.*, ET p. 130 (German p. lxxxv).
112. *Ibid.*, ET p. 131 (German p. lxxxvi).
113. *Ibid.*, ET p. 143 (German p. xcii).
114. H. Gunkel, 'Jacob', *Preussische Jahrbücher*, 176 (1919), pp. 339-62, ET 'Jacob' in *What Remains of the Old Testament* (New York, 1928), pp. 150-86.
115. *Ibid.*, ET p. 172 (German p. 353).

116. *Ibid.*, ET p. 180 (German p. 358).
117. *Ibid.*, ET p. 174 (German p. 354).
118. *Ibid.*, ET p. 174 (German p. 354).
119. *Ibid.*, ET p. 170 (German p. 352).
120. *Ibid.*, ET p. 185 (German p. 362).
121. *Ibid.*, ET p. 186 (German p. 362).
122. *Ibid.*, ET p. 186 (German p. 362).
123. *Ibid.*, ET p. 186 (German p. 362).
124. *Ibid.*, ET p. 168 (German p. 351).
125. *Ibid.*, ET p. 185 (German p. 362).
126. *Ibid.*, ET pp. 158-63 (German pp. 345-48).
127. J. Van Seters, *Abraham in History and Tradition* (New Haven and London, 1975), p. 133, fails to take into account this later position of Gunkel, which admits that aetiological statements are 'almost always secondary'. See W. McKane, *Studies in the Patriarchal Narratives* (Edinburgh, 1979), pp. 43-47, which incorporates a slight modification of the position taken by W. Klatt, *op. cit.*, pp. 136ff.
128. 'Tradition' is used here in the sense defined by D.A. Knight, *Rediscovering the Traditions of Israel* (SBL Dissertations 9; Missoula, 1973), p. 26, i.e. as that which (i) has been received from others and handed down from generation to generation; (ii) is the property of a group; (iii) is living, developing and only relatively stable; (iv) is usually oral but can be in written form as long as it can still develop and adapt; and (v) tends to be accumulative and agglomerative. Cf. J. Vansina's definition of oral tradition in *Oral Tradition as History* (London, 1985), pp. 27f.
129. *Contra* K. Koch, *The Growth of the Biblical Tradition* (ET from the 2nd German edn, London, 1969), p. 66, who reserves the term 'tradition-historical' for those Scandinavian scholars whose sole interest in the biblical text has been with the history of its oral transmission.
130. A. Alt, 'Der Gott der Väter, *Kleine Schriften zur Geschichte des Volkes Israel*, I (München, 1959), pp. 1-78. ET 'The God of the Fathers' in *Essays on Old Testament History and Religion* (Oxford, 1966), pp. 1-66.
131. *Ibid.*, ET p. 6 (German p. 4).
132. *Ibid.*, ET p. 10 (German p. 9).
133. *Ibid.*, ET p. 50 (German p. 49).
134. *Ibid.*, ET p. 50 (German pp. 50-51).
135. *Ibid.*, ET p. 55 (German p. 56).
136. J. Van Seters, *op. cit.*, pp. 141-42.
137. A. Alt, *op. cit.*, p. 23.
138. ET, *Genesis* (OTL; London, 1972), p. 13 = G. von Rad, *Genesis* (9th edn; Göttingen, 1972), p. 2.
139. ET, *The Problem of the Hexateuch and Other Essays* (Edinburgh, 1966), pp. 1-74 = *Das formgeschichtliche Problem des Hexateuch* (BWANT 26; Stuttgart, 1938), reprinted in *Gesammelte Studien zum Alten Testament*

(München, 1958), pp. 9-86.
140. *Ibid.*, ET p. 2 (German pp. 10f.).
141. *Ibid.*, ET p. 4 (German p. 12).
142. *Ibid.*, ET p. 8 (German pp. 14f.).
143. *Ibid.*, ET p. 13 (German p. 20).
144. *Ibid.*, ET p. 18 (German pp. 25-27).
145. *Ibid.*, ET pp. 42-46 (Geman pp. 42-46).
146. *Ibid.*, ET p. 50 (German pp. 57f.).
147. *Ibid.*, ET p. 66 (German pp. 71f.).
148. G. von Rad, ET, *Genesis*, p. 22 (German p. 8).
149. *Ibid.*, ET p. 22 (German p. 8).
150. *Ibid.*, ET p. 31 (German p. 16).
151. *Ibid.*, ET p. 32 (German p. 17), 'the tyranny of history is in fact able to assert of the saga that it simply does not exist but is only a kind of timid preparation for history itself'.
152. *Ibid.*, ET p. 33 (German p. 17).
153. *Ibid.*, ET p. 33 (German p. 18).
154. *Ibid.*, ET p. 33 (German p. 18).
155. *Ibid.*, ET p. 34 (German p. 18).
156. *Ibid.*, ET p. 34 (German p. 19). Chapter 3 will discuss von Rad's adoption here of Westermann's use of Jolles' theories of genre development.
157. *Ibid.*, ET p. 35 (German p. 19).
158. *Ibid.*, ET p. 36 (German p. 20).
159. *Ibid.*, ET p. 37 (German p. 21).
160. *Ibid.*, ET p. 40 (German p. 24).
161. A more detailed presentation of the matter will be pursued in Chapter 3, where the influence of folklore studies on genre distinctions will be discussed.
162. See B.S. Childs, 'Deuteronomic Formulae of the Exodus Traditions', *Hebräische Wortforschung*, Festschrift für W. Baumgartner (SVT 16; Leiden, 1967), pp. 30-39. For a concise résumé of the issues involved see also E.W. Nicholson, *Exodus and Sinai in History and Tradition* (London, 1973), pp. 20-21.
163. M. Noth, *Überlieferungsgeschichte des Pentateuch* (Stuttgart, 1948). ET *A History of Pentateuchal Traditions* (London, 1968).
164. *Ibid.*, ET p. 46 (German p. 50).
165. *Ibid.*, ET pp. 47-51 (German pp. 50-54).
166. *Ibid.*, ET pp. 51-54 (German pp. 54-58).
167. *Ibid.*, ET pp. 54-58 (German pp. 58-62).
168. *Ibid.*, ET pp. 58-59 (German pp. 62-67).
169. *Ibid.*, ET pp. 59-67 (German pp. 63-67).
170. *Ibid.*, ET p. 190 (German p. 207).
171. *Ibid.*, ET p. 276 (German p. 276).
172. *Ibid.*, ET pp. 50f. (German p. 53).

173. *Ibid.*, ET pp. 38-41 (German pp. 40-44).
174. *Ibid.*, ET p. 62 (German p. 67).
175. *Ibid.*, ET p. 62 (German p. 67).
176. *Ibid.*, ET p. 62 (German p. 67).
177. *Ibid.*, ET p. 62 (German p. 67).
178. *Ibid.*, ET p. 64 (German p. 69).
179. *Ibid.*, ET p. 197 (German p. 215).
180. *Ibid.*, ET p. 231 (German p. 251).
181. *Ibid.*, ET pp. 231f. (German p. 250).
182. *Ibid.*, ET p. 44 (German p. 47).
183. *Ibid.*, ET p. 56 (German p. 59).
184. *Ibid.*, ET p. 57 (German p. 60).
185. For the most recent attempt to show that the promise to Jacob in Genesis 28 is integral to the narrative at its oral stage of composition see A. de Pury, *Promesse Divine et légende cultuelle dans le cycle de Jacob: Genèse 28 et les traditions patriarcales* (Paris, 1975), pp. 345-470. Cf. also J.A. Emerton, 'The Origin of the Promises to the Patriarchs in the Older Sources of the Book of Genesis', *VT* 32 (1982), pp. 14-32, who, *contra* de Pury, maintains that Gen. 28.10-22 is not a unity and that Gen. 28.14 is a secondary addition.
186. M. Noth, *op. cit.*, ET p. 44 (German p. 47); G. von Rad, ET *Genesis* p. 17 (German p. 8).
187. C.H. De Geus, *The Tribes of Israel* (Amsterdam, 1976); A.D.H. Mayes, 'The Period of the Judges and the Rise of the Monarchy', in *Israelite and Judean History*, ed. J.H. Hayes and J.M. Miller (London, 1977), pp. 229-308.
188. S. Thompson, *The Folktale* (London, 1946), pp. 437-42.
189. F.C. Bartlett, 'Some Experiments on the Reproduction of Folk Stories', *Folklore* 31 (1920), pp. 30-47; *idem*, *Remembering* (Cambridge, 1932), *passim*.
190. R.H. Lowie, 'Oral Tradition and History', *JAF* 30 (1917), pp. 161-67.
191. R. Finnegan, *Oral Poetry* (London, 1977), pp. 30-41; J.M. Ellis, *One Fairy Story Too Many* (London, 1983), esp. pp. 25-28, where Ellis describes the questioning of romantic theories with regard to the editorial techniques and sources of the brothers Grimm.
192. D.A. Knight, *op. cit.*, pp. 217-399.
193. *Ibid.*, pp. 218-19.
194. H.S. Nyberg, *Studien zum Hoseabuche: Zugleich ein Beitrag zur Klärung des Problems der alttestamentlichen Textkritik* (Uppsala, 1935); *idem*, 'Das Textkritische demonstriert', *ZAW* 52 (1934), pp. 242-46.
195. Nyberg, *op. cit.*, p. 245.
196. *Ibid.*, p. 245.
197. *Ibid.*, p. 245.

198. *Ibid.*, p. 246.
199. H. Birkeland, *Zum hebräischen Traditionswesen: Die Komposition der prophetischen Bücher des Alten Testaments* (Oslo, 1938), p. 78.
200. *Ibid.*, pp. 7-12.
201. *Ibid.*, p. 13.
202. *Ibid.*, p. 20.
203. *Ibid.*, pp. 22f.
204. Engnell's *Gamla Testamentet* has never been translated, but many of his methodological presuppositions are spelled out in a collection of his articles in *Critical Essays on the Old Testament*, trans. and ed. J.T. Willis and H. Ringgren (London, 1970).
205. I. Engnell, 'The Traditio-historical Method in Old Testament Research', *ibid.*, p. 3.
206. *Ibid.*, p. 6.
207. *Ibid.*, p. 7.
208. *Ibid.*, p. 9.
209. *Ibid.*, p. 11.
210. I. Engnell, 'The Pentateuch', *op. cit.*, pp. 50-67, esp. p. 54.
211. *Ibid.*, p. 54.
212. *Ibid.*, pp. 54-58.
213. *Ibid.*, pp. 58-59.
214. *Ibid.*, p. 61.
215. *Ibid.*, p. 63.
216. *Ibid.*, pp. 65-66.
217. G. Widengren, *Literary and Psychological Aspects of the Hebrew Prophets* (Uppsala, 1948).
218. *Ibid.*, pp. 35-45.
219. *Ibid.*, p. 58.
220. G. Widengren, 'Oral Tradition and Written Literature among the Hebrews in the Light of Arabic Evidence, with Special Regard to Prose Narratives', *Acta Orientalia* 23 (1959), pp. 201-62.
221. E. Nielson, *Oral Tradition: A Modern Problem in Old Testament Introduction* (SBT 11; London, 1954), pp. 36f.
222. *Ibid.*, p. 37.
223. S. Thompson, *op. cit.*, p. 456.

Notes to Chapter 2

1. R.C. Culley, *Oral Formulaic Language in the Biblical Psalms* (Toronto, 1967); I. Ljung, *Tradition and Interpretation* (Uppsala, 1978).
2. M. Parry, 'The Homeric Language as the Language of an Oral Poetry', *Harvard Studies in Classical Philology* 43 (1932), pp. 1-50.
3. A.B. Lord, *The Singer of Tales* (New York, 1960).

4. *Ibid.*, p. 17.
5. *Ibid.*, p. 44.
6. *Ibid.*, pp. 54-57.
7. *Ibid.*, p. 58.
8. *Ibid.*, p. 68.
9. *Ibid.*, p. 94
10. *Ibid.*, p. 101.
11. *Ibid.*, p. 101.
12. *Ibid.*, p. 131.
13. L.D. Benson, 'The Literary Character of Anglo-Saxon Formulaic Poetry', *PMLA* 81 (1966), pp. 334-71.
14. J. Opland, '"Scop" and "Imbongi"—Anglo-Saxon and Bantu Oral Poets', *English Studies in Africa* 14 (1971), pp. 161-78; *idem*, *Anglo-Saxon Oral Poetry* (Michigan, 1980), p. 76, where Opland criticizes Lord, pointing out his admission that a low frequency of formulae may be 'the product of a highly talented poet'.
15. R. Finnegan, *Oral Poetry* (London, 1979), pp. 73-75.
16. A. Jabbour, 'Memorial Transmission in Old English Poetry', *The Chaucer Review* 3 (1969), pp. 174-90.
17. R. Finnegan, *op. cit.*, p. 86.
18. A.B. Lord, 'A Comparative Analysis', in *Umbundu: Folktales from Angola*, compiled and translated by M. Ennis (Boston, 1962), pp. i-xxv.
19. *Ibid.*, p. xiii.
20. *Ibid.*, p. xxix.
21. A.B. Lord, 'Perspectives on Recent Work on Oral Literature', in *Oral Literature: Seven Essays*, ed. J.J. Duggan (London, 1975), p. 19.
22. *Ibid.*, p. 18.
23. A.B. Lord, 'Memory, Fixity and Genre in Oral Traditional Poetries', in *Oral Traditional Literature: A Festschrift for A.B. Lord*, ed. J.M. Foley (Ohio, 1981), p. 460.
24. *Ibid.*, p. 459.
25. A.B. Lord, 'The Gospels as Oral Traditional Literature', in *The Relationship Among the Gospels*, ed. W.D. Walker Jr (San Antonio, 1978), p. 37.
26. *Ibid.*, p. 37.
27. R. Finnegan, *Oral Literature in Africa* (Oxford, 1970), pp. 354-86.
28. H. Lloyd-Jones, 'Remarks on the Homeric Question', in *History and Imagination*, ed. H. Lloyd-Jones, V. Pearl and B. Worden (London, 1981), pp. 15-29.
29. See p. 25.
30. Cf. A.B. Lord, 'A Comparative Analysis' *op. cit.*, p. xvi.
31. R. Finnegan, *Oral Poetry*, p. 130.
32. D. Tannen, 'Oral and Literate Strategies in Spoken and Written Narratives', *Language* 58 (1982), pp. 1-21.

Notes to Chapter 2

33. J. Van Seters, *Abraham in History and Tradition* (London, 1975).
34. A. Olrik, 'Epische Gesetze der Volksdichtung', *Zeitschrift für Deutsches Altertum* 51 (1909), pp. 1-12.
35. When F.W. Schmidt embarked upon a study of the legend he found it impossible to rely upon already existing transcripts. He therefore found it necessary to collect his own oral narrative material in the field. Cf. F.W. Schmidt, 'Die Volkssage als Kuntswerk', in *Vergleichende Sagenforschung*, ed. L. Petzoldt (Darmstadt, 1969), pp. 21-65, originally in *Niederdeutsche Zeitschrift in Volkskunde* 7 (1929), pp. 129-43.
36. L. Dégh and A. Vazsonyi, 'The Memorate and the Proto Memorate', *JAF* 87 (1974), pp. 233f.
37. D. Tedlock, 'Toward an Oral Poetics', *NLH* 8 (1977), p. 509.
38. L. Danielson, 'Toward the Analysis of Vernacular Texts: The Supernatural Narrative in Oral and Popular Print Sources', *Journal of the Folklore Institute* 16 (1979), p. 141.
39. J. Pentikäinen, 'Repertoire Analysis', in *Folk Narrative Research*, ed. J. Pentikäinen (Helsinki, 1976), p. 270.
40. *Idem*, 'Oral Transmission of Knowledge', in *Folklore in the Modern World*, ed. R. Dorson (Paris, 1978), pp. 237-52. 'In distinct contrast to what Olrik supposes most epic laws did not seem—at least on the basis of Takalo's material—to apply to all narrative genres' (p. 248).
41. *Idem*, *Oral Repertoire and World View* (Helsinki, 1978), p. 295.
42. J. Van Seters, *op. cit.*, pp. 154-55.
43. *Ibid.*, pp. 157-59.
44. *Ibid.*, p. 160.
45. *Ibid.*, p. 161.
46. A. Olrik, *op. cit.*, p. 4.
47. R. Kellogg, 'Oral Narrative Written Book', *Genre* 10 (1977), p. 662.
48. A.B. Lord, 'A Comparative Analysis', pp. xiii-xvi.
49. For 'The Vampire' see ed. F.H. Groom, *Gypsy Folktales* (Pennsylvania, 1963), pp. 14-18.
50. For 'Pretty Maid Ibronka' see ET, trans. J. Halasz, ed. L. Dégh, *Folktales of Hungary* (Chicago, 1965), pp. 46-57.
51. B. Gray, 'Repetition in Oral Literature', *JAF* 84 (1971), p. 303.
52. *Ibid.*, p. 289.
53. Van Seters, *op. cit.*, pp. 162-63.
54. Van Seters, *op. cit.*, p. 163.
55. Cf. A.B. Lord, *op. cit.* (1978), p. 43, also S.M. Warner, 'Primitive Saga Men', *VT* 39 (1979), pp. 325-35; and my own comments on equating simplicity of form with simplicity of ancient mentality, pp. 28-29.
56. See now A.B. Lord's warning in 'Memory Fixity and Genre', in *Oral Tradition Poetries in Oral Traditional Literature*, p. 459.
57. J. Van Seters, *op. cit.*, p. 163.
58. B. Gray, *op. cit.*, p. 297, 'The appearance of a particular motif or tale

type in a work provides per se no evidence whatsoever as to the oral or written provenance of the work'.
59. J. Van Seters, *op. cit.*, p. 191.
60. *Ibid.*, p. 313.
61. *Ibid.*, p. 161.
62. W.J. Ong, *Orality and Literacy* (London, 1982), pp. 31-75.
63. J. Goody, *The Domestication of the Savage Mind* (London, 1977), pp. 1-51.
64. D. Tannen, 'Oral and Literate Strategies in Spoken and Written Narratives', *Language* 58 (1982), p. 2 n. 3.
65. R. Finnegan, *op. cit.*, p. 127.
66. *Ibid.*, p. 133. For a discussion on the aspect of performance see also pp. 118-26.
67. *Ibid.*, p. 132; *contra* R. Knierim, who argues for a 'qualitative difference between oral and written language' but offers no substantiation in 'Old Testament Form Criticism Reconsidered', *Int* 27 (1973), p. 257.
68. J. Van Seters, *op. cit.*, p. 161.
69. *Ibid.*, p. 162.
70. K. Koch, *The Growth of the Biblical Tradition*, ET, S.M. Cupit (2nd edn, New York, 1969), p. 91 n. 47.
71. J. Pentikäinen, *Oral Repertoire and World View* (Helsinki, 1978).
72. C.W. von Sydow, *Selected Papers on Folklore*, ed. L. Bodken (Copenhagen, 1948), p. 12.
73. L. Dégh, *Folktales and Society: Telling in a Hungarian Peasant Community* (Indiana, 1969), p. 179.
74. J. Pentaiäinen, 'Oral Transmission of Knowledge', in *Folklore in the Modern World*, ed. R.M. Dorson (Paris, 1978), p. 242.
75. *Ibid.*, p. 250.
76. J. Pentikäinen, 'Repertoire Analysis', in *Folk Narrative Research*, ed. J. Pentikäinen (Helsinki, 1976), p. 296.
77. J. Pentikäinen, *Oral Repertoire and World View* (Helsinki, 1978), p. 57.
78. *Ibid.*, p. 20.
79. So Birkeland's examples of Koranic readings or Nielson's example of a blind student's accurate recitation of Vedic literature.
80. R. Finnegan, *Oral Poetry* (London, 1979), p. 141.
81. M. Noth, ET *A History of Pentateuchal Traditions* (Englewood Cliffs, 1972), p. 103 = *Überlieferungsgeschichte des Pentateuch* (Stuttgart, 1948), p. 113; cf. K. Koch, *op. cit.*, p. 126.
82. J.R. Moore, 'The Influence of Transmission on the English Ballad', in *Modern Language Review* 11 (1916), p. 387, as quoted in D.J. McMillan, 'A Survey of Theories Concerning the Oral Transmission of the Traditional Ballad', *Southern Folklore Quarterly* 28 (1964), p. 301.
83. R. Finnegan, *op. cit.*, pp. 142-53; R.C. Culley, *Studies in the Structure*

of *Hebrew Narrative* (Missoula, 1976), pp. 30-31.
84. R. Finnegan, *op. cit.*, pp. 142-43.
85. G.L. Ritteridge, *Francis James Child's English and Scottish Popular Ballads* (Boston, 1932), p. xvii.
86. So Engnell.
87. R. Finnegan, *op. cit.*, p. 153.
88. G. Ortutay, 'Principles of Oral Transmission in Folk Culture', *Acta Ethnographica* 8 (1959), p. 188.
89. D. Tedlock, 'The Spoken Word and the Work of Interpretation in American Indian Religion', in *Traditional Literatures of the American Indian*, ed. K. Kroeber (London, 1981), pp. 45-59.
90. *Ibid.*, p. 48.
91. So A.B. Lord, *The Singer of Tales*, p. 137.
92. R. Finnegan, *op. cit.*, pp. 161-63.
93. *Ibid.*, p. 168; cf. Engnell's position, pp. 47-48.
94. R.C. Culley, *op. cit.*, p. 31.
95. *Ibid.*, p. 67.

Notes to Chapter 3

1. See pp. 54, 68.
2. *Contra* J. Barton, who argues that both source and form criticism arose independently of other disciplines. 'The techniques of source and form criticism, at any rate, were developed by biblical scholars for biblical studies, rather than being taken over from other disciplines' (*Reading the Old Testament* [London, 1984], p. 155).
3. H. Gunkel, *Genesis* (Göttingen, 1910), pp. xxvii-xxviii.
4. *Ibid.*, p. xii.
5. F.M. Cross, *Canaanite Myth and Hebrew Epic* (Cambridge, MA, 1973); cf. esp. p. 124 n. 38, where appeal to an oral Homeric epic tradition is made.
6. For the most recent discussion and historical survey of the use of the concept of myth in the Old Testament see J.W. Rogerson, *Myth in Old Testament Interpretation* (Berlin, 1974).
7. R.D. Abrahams, 'The Complex Relations in Simple Forms', *Genre* 2 (1969), p. 104.
8. T. Todorov, *Les Genres du Discours* (Paris, 1978), p. 51. For a more recent discussion see J. Vansina, *Oral Tradition as History* (London, 1985), p. 81.
9. *Ibid.*, p. 51.
10. A. Dundes, 'Texture, Text, and Context', *SFQ* 28 (1964), p. 252.
11. S.K.D. Stahl, 'Narrative Genres: A Question of Academic Assumptions', *Fabula* 21 (1980), p. 83; R. Knierim, 'Old Testament Form Criticism Reconsidered', *Int* 27 (1973), p. 436.

12. Most recently B.S. Childs, *Introduction to the Old Testament as Scripture* (London, 1979), p. 115.

13. The confusion is now compounded by W. McKane, who, following W.F. Albright, adopts the term saga in his otherwise masterful presentation of the history of biblical criticism on the patriarchal narratives in *Studies in the Patriarchal Narratives* (Edinburgh, 1979), p. 18; see also Albright's introduction to H. Gunkel, *The Legends of Israel*, ET by W.H. Carruth (London, 1966), p. ix; cf. J.H. Hayes in *Old Testament Form Criticism* (Trinity, 1974), p. 59, where he translates *Sage* as saga. More recently in *An Introduction to Old Testament Study* (Nashville, 1979), p. 130, he translates the term as legend.

14. *Oxford English Dictionary* (Oxford, 1971).

15. T.M. Anderson, 'The Icelandic Sagas', in *Heroic Epic and Saga*, ed. F.J. Onias (London, 1978), pp. 144-51.

16. So also G.B. Caird, *The Language and Imagery of the Bible* (London, 1980), p. 204.

17. Saga is distinguished on these grounds by G.M. Tucker in *Form Criticism of the Old Testament* (Philadelphia, 1971), p. 38.

18. For a discussion of the problems of translation cf. P. Gilbert, 'Légende ou Saga?', *VT* 24 (1974), pp. 411-20.

19. J.L.C. and W.C. Grimm, *Kinder- und Hausmärchen* (Leipzig, 1812-1815).

20. J.L.C. and W.C. Grimm, *Deutsche Sagen* (Berlin, 1816-1818).

21. J.L.C. Grimm, *Deutsche Mythologie* (Göttingen, 1835).

22. J.L.C. Grimm, ET *Teutonic Mythology*, III (London, 1884) pp. xiii-xvii.

23. J. Zipes, *Fairy Tales and the Art of Subversion* (London, 1983), pp. 49-51.

24. *Ibid.*, p. 56.

25. Wesselski's emphasis on the written text, ridiculed by S. Thompson, *The Folktale* (London, 1946 repr. 1977), pp. 441-42, would now seem to be justified.

26. J.M. Ellis, *One Fairy Story Too Many* (London, 1983), pp. 81f.

27. *Ibid.*, p. 27. See also C. Dollerup, I. Reventlow, C.R. Hansen, 'A Case Study of Editorial Filters in Folktales: A Discussion of the Allerleirauh Tales in Grimm', *Fabula* 27 (1986), where it is argued that 'discussions of recorded tales should take into account later filters and orientations' (p. 28).

28. *Ibid.*, p. 89. See C. Dollerup, I. Reventlow, C.R. Hansen, *op. cit.*, p. 29, who attempt to defend the brothers Grimm against Ellis' disclosures. Unfortunately, arguments such as the following are unconvincing: 'We know that virtually all the brothers' informants were middle-class people, but in many tales... there is a layer of non-middle class norms, and these norms could not have originated in a Bourgeois milieu'.

29. *Ibid.*, pp. 35f.
30. G.L. Gomme, *Folklore as an Historical Science* (London, 1908), p. 129.
31. J. Frazer, *Apollodorus*, I (New York, 1921), pp. 27f.
32. As is pointed out in the preface and introduction to the 2nd edn of *Morphology of the Folktale*, the title is an incorrect translation and should read fairy tale. In 'Structure and History in the Study of the Fairy Tale', *Semeia* 14 (1978), pp. 57-83—a translation of his 1928 article—V. Propp suggests (p. 69) that it would have been better to entitle the book *The Composition of the Fairy Tale in Folklore*.
33. V. Propp, 'Structure and History in the Study of the Fairy Tale', *ibid.*, p. 71.
34. See pp. 160f.; cf. also D. Ben-Amos, 'Analytical Categories and Ethnic Genres', *Genre* 2 (1969), p. 277, where he states that Märchen are absent from the Bible.
35. R. Barthes, 'La Lutte avec l'ange: analyse textuelle de Genèse 32.23-33', in *Analyse structurelle et exégèse biblique*, ed. R. Barthes and F. Bovon (Neuchatel, 1971), pp. 27-40.
36. A. Dundes, *The Morphology of North American Indian Folktales* (FFC 195; Helsinki, 1964).
37. J. Pentikäinen, *Oral Repertoire and World View* (Helsinki, 1978), pp. 287-89.
38. A. Jolles, *Einfache Formen* (Halle, 1929, reprinted Tübingen, 1968).
39. In the recent work of J. Van Seters, *Abraham in History and Tradition* (London, 1975), pp. 135f., A. Jolles' position is quite properly criticized.
40. *Op. cit.*, p. 8.
41. *Ibid.*, p. 10.
42. *Ibid.*, p. 63.
43. *Ibid.*, p. 65.
44. *Ibid.*, p. 68.
45. *Ibid.*, p. 75.
46. *Ibid.*, pp. 87-88.
47. F.L. Utley, 'Oral Genres as Bridge to Written Literature', *Acta Ethnographica* 19 (1970), pp. 389-91.
48. T.M. Andersson, 'The Icelandic Sagas', in *Heroic Epic and Saga*, ed. F.J. Oinas (London, 1978), pp. 149-51.
49. *Ibid.*, p. 43.
50. C.W. von Sydow, 'Katagorien der Prosa-Volksdichtung', in *Selected Papers on Folklore* (Copenhagen, 1948), pp. 61-64.
51. This criticism is similar to Warner's strictures that Gunkel's romantic views of 'Primitive Saga Men' and their primitive minds, were based on psychological prejudices which not only could not be verified but are quite simply incorrect. Cf. 'Primitive Saga Men', *VT* 29 (1979), pp. 256-64.
52. C. Westermann, *The Promise of the Fathers*, ET (Philadeplhia, 1980),

p. 32, from *Die Verheissungen an die Väter* (Göttingen, 1976), p. 36.
53. *Ibid.*, ET p. 75 (German p. 89).
54. C. Westermann, ET *Genesis 12–36: A Commentary* (London, 1986) p. 107 = *Genesis* (BKAT 1/2; Neukirchen-Vluyn, 1980), p. 74.
55. *Ibid.*, ET p. 79 (German p. 81).
56. *Ibid.*, ET p. 577 (German p. 703).
57. K. Ranke, 'Einfache Formen', *JFI* 4/1 (1967), pp. 17-31.
58. C.W. von Sydow, *op. cit.*, pp. 60-85.
59. S. Thompson, *Motif Index of Folk Literature* (Helsinki, 1932-1936), Vols. I-IV (new edn; Copenhagen, 1955, 1958), p. 11.
60. S. Thompson, *The Folktale* (London, 1946), p. 4.
61. *Ibid.*, p. 8.
62. *Ibid.*, p. 8.
63. *Ibid.*, p. 10.
64. *Ibid.*, pp. 447-48.
65. O. Eissfeldt, *The Old Testament. An Introduction*, ET Peter R. Ackroyd (Oxford, 1965), pp. 37-47, from the German *Einleitung in das Alte Testament*, 3rd edn (Tübingen, 1964), pp. 48-54.
66. *Ibid.*, ET p. 34 (German p. 44).
67. *Ibid.*, ET p. 48 (German p. 63).
68. O. Eissfeldt, 'Stammessage und Menschheitserzählung in der Genesis', *Sitzungsberichte der sächsischen Akademie der Wissenschaften zu Leipzig*, Band 110/4 (1965), pp. 5-26; for a critical assessment of the notion of corporate personality see J.W. Rogerson, 'The Hebrew Conception of Corporate Personality: A Re-examination', *JTS* 21 (1970), pp. 1-16.
69. O. Eissfeldt, 'Genesis', *The Interpreter's Dictionary of the Bible*, Vol. II (1962), p. 372.
70. O. Eissfeldt, 'Achronische, anachronische und synchronische Elemente in der Genesis', Jaarbericht van het Vooraziatischegyptisch Genootschap, *Ex Oriente Lux* 17 (1963), pp. 161f.
71. W.R. Bascom, 'The Forms of Folklore: Prose Narratives', *JAF* 78 (1965), p. 3.
72. *Ibid.*, pp. 4f.
73. R. Finnegan, *Limba Stories and Story Telling* (Oxford, 1967), pp. 42-48.
74. R.D. Abrahams, *op. cit.*, (1969), p. 110.
75. D. Ben-Amos. 'Analytical Categories and Ethnic Genres', *Genre* 2 (1969), p. 273.
76. D. Ben-Amos, 'Introduction: Folklore in African Society, in *Forms of Folklore in Africa*, ed. B. Lindfors (London, 1977), p. 3.
77. D. Ben-Amos, *op. cit.*, p. 297. For an example of culturally determined genres within European tradition, cf. J. Pentikäinen, *op. cit.*, p. 301.
78. See V. Voigt, 'Towards a Theory of Genres in Folklore', in *Folklore Today*, ed. L. Dégh, H. Glassie and F. Oinas (Bloomington, 1976), p. 490.
79. R.D. Abrahams, *op. cit.*, p. 125; D. Ben-Amos, 'Toward a Definition of

Folklore in Context', *JAF* 84 (1971), p. 10.
80. L. Dégh, 'Folk Narrative', in *Folklore and Folklife*, ed. R.M. Dorson (Chicago, 1972), p. 59.
81. *Ibid.*, p. 59.
82. D. Ben-Amos, 'Introduction ...', p. 7. Also cf. pp. 9-12, in which he discusses the significance of opening and closing formulae for establishing genre.
83. See pp. 66-68, where Olrik's attempts to establish orality on the basis of universally binding laws of folk narrative composition are criticized.
84. D. Irvin, *Mytharion: The Comparison of Tales from the Old Testament and the Ancient Near East* (Neukirchen, 1978).
85. *Ibid.*, p. 3.
86. *Ibid.*, p. 10.
87. Pp. 79-83.
88. See plot-motif and traditional episode table in D. Irving, *op. cit.*, appendix (n.p.).
89. *Ibid.*, p. 113.
90. H. Jason, *Ethnopoetry* (Bonn, 1977), p. 6.
91. *Ibid.*, p. 13.
92. *Ibid.*, pp. 9-13.
93. *Ibid.*, p. 13.
94. *Ibid.*, p. 17.
95. *Ibid.*, p. 24.
96. *Ibid.*, p. 25.
97. *Ibid.*, pp. 27-32.
98. *Ibid.*, pp. 33-36.
99. *Ibid.*, pp. 38-40.
100. *Ibid.*, pp. 42, 43.
101. *Ibid.*, pp. 9-12; cf. J. Pentikäinen, *Oral Repertoire*, pp. 269f.; see also V. Propp's Structure and History in the Study of the Fairy-Tale', *Semeia* 11 (1978), p. 82, which suggests that myth precedes the fairy tale because it is impossible to have a fairy tale with a similar plot to myth when belief in the myth still exists.
102. F.M. Cross, *op. cit.*, p. viii.
103. Cf. W.F. Albright's discussion of oral transmission in *From Stone Age to Christianity* (Baltimore, 1959), p. 66, where he states, 'it is generally recognized that the verse form is much better adapted for oral transmission ... our present prose form of an orally transmitted document is the result of a secondary adaption or abstraction'.
104. H. Jason, 'The Story of David and Goliath: A Folk Epic', *Biblica* 60 (1979), p. 36.
105. She is also dependent on V. Propp.
106. H. Jason, *op. cit.*, p. 37.
107. H. Jason, *ibid.*, pp. 38f.

108. H. Finnegan, *Oral Poetry* (Cambridge, 1979), p. 98, also pp. 99-109.

109. H. Jason, *op. cit.*, p. 40.

110. *Ibid.*, pp. 43-47. Jason also offers an obscure analysis of the significance of numbers found in the text, which she argues provides evidence of a unified narrative (pp. 47f.).

111. *Ibid., contra*, pp. 61-70.

112. I am aware that central to the definitions of Jason's genre classification is that of orality, but a text's prior oral form cannot be argued on the basis of genre definition.

113. Cf. C. Conroy, 'Hebrew Epic: Historical Notes and Critical Reflections', *Biblica* 61 (1980), p. 29; also S. Talmon, 'The Comparative Method in Biblical Interpretation—Principles and Problems', *VTS* 29 (1978), p. 356.

114. H. Jason and A. Kempinski, 'How Old are Folktales?', *Fabula* 22 (1981), pp. 1-21. Folktale in this context is used to signify all oral narrative genres.

115. *Ibid.*, p. 3.
116. *Ibid.*, p. 6.
117. *Ibid.*, p. 4.
118. *Ibid.*, p. 4.
119. *Ibid.*, p. 4.
120. *Ibid.*, pp. 12f.
121. *Ibid.*, p. 3.

122. For an excellent study on the topic, see J. Van Seters, *In Search of History* (London 1983).

123. T. Todorov, *Les Genres du Discours* (Paris, 1978), p. 47, 'Un nouveau genre est toujours la transformation d'un ou de plusieurs genres anciens'.

124. J. Van Seters, *op. cit.*.

125. H. Gunkel, *Legends, op. cit.*, p. 6; *Genesis* (Göttingen, 1910), p. x.

126. *Ibid.*, ET p. 10 (German p. xii).
127. *Ibid.*, ET p. 10 (German p. xii).
128. *Ibid.*, ET p. 10 (German p. xi)
129. *Ibid.*, ET p. 11 (German p. xii).
130. *Ibid.*, ET p. 22 (German p. xviii).
131. *Ibid.*, ET p. 74 (German p. xlviii).
132. *Ibid.*, ET pp. 132f. (German p. lxxxvi).
133. *Ibid.*, ET p. 23 (German p. xx).
134. *Ibid.*, ET p. 23 (German p. xx).
135. *Ibid.*, ET p. 24 (German p. xx).

136. *Ibid.*, ET p. 24. N.B. In the first edition the example used is that of Jacob and Esau; in the 3rd edition the example of ethnographic legends had changed to those of Cain and of Ishmael (*ibid.*, p. xx).

137. *Ibid.*, ET p. 22 (German p. xix).

138. See T.L. Thompson, 'Conflict Themes in the Jacob Narratives', *Semeia* 15 (1979), pp. 5-26.
139. See R.C. Culley, 'Oral Tradition and Historicity', in *Studies in the Ancient Palestinian World*, ed. J. Wevers and D. Redford (Toronto, 1972), pp. 106-16.
140. R.C. Culley, *ibid.*, pp. 111-15.
141. J. Vansina, *De la tradition orale: Essai de méthode historique* (Paris, 1961).
142. See preface to the ET (by H.M. Wright) of J. Vansina, *Oral Tradition* (Aylesbury, 1973), p. xiv.
143. *Ibid.*, pp. xii-xiv.
144. *Ibid.*, p. xiv.
145. *Ibid.*, p. 155.
146. *Ibid.*, p. 171.
147. *Ibid.*, p. 171.
148. *Ibid.*, p. 172.
149. D.P. Henige, 'Oral Tradition and Chronology', *Journal of African History* 12 (1971), p. 389; idem, *The Chronology of Oral Tradition* (Oxford, 1974), pp. 55f.
150. R.M. Dorson, 'Oral Tradition and Written History: The Case for the United States', *JFK* 1 (1964), p. 230.
151. L. Duprée, 'The Retreat of the British Army from Kabul to Jalalabad in 1842: History and Folklore', *JFK* 4 (1967), pp. 50-74.
152. J. Vansina, *op. cit.*, p. xiv.
153. J.C. Miller, *Kings and Kinsmen* (Oxford, 1976), p. 23.
154. *Ibid.*, p. 13.
155. *Ibid.*, pp. 26-27.
156. See P. Irwin, *Liptako Speaks* (Princeton, 1980); D.R. Wright, *Oral Traditions from the Gambia*, Vol. I (Ohio, 1979); D.P. Henige, *The Chronology of Oral Tradition* (Oxford, 1974); G. Innes, *Felefa Saane: His Career Recounted by Two Mandinka Bards* (London, 1978).
157. J. Vansina, *The Children of Woot: A History of the Kuba People* (Folkestone, 1978), p. 77.
158. In this respect the *Malunda* are comparable to the 'core clichés of Xhosa *'ntsomi* which are analyzed by H. Scheub in 'The Technique of the Expansible Image in Xhosa Ntsomi-Performances', ed. B. Lindfors, *Forms of Folklore in Africa* (London, 1977), pp. 37-63. H. Scheub's work is also summarized by R.C. Culley in *Studies in the Structure of Hebrew Narrative* (Philadelphia, 1976), pp. 13-16.
159. J.C. Miller, *op. cit.*, p. 23.
160. *Ibid.*, p. 12.
161. *Ibid.*, p. 13.
162. *Ibid.*, p. 25.
163. R. Finnegan, 'A Note on Oral Tradition and Historical Evidence',

History and Theory 9 (1970), p. 197.

164. J. Vansina, *Oral Tradition*, p. 153.
165. R. Finnegan, *op. cit.*, p. 199.
166. R.R. Wilson, *Genealogy and History in the Biblical World* (New Haven and London, 1977), p. 54.
167. D.R. Wright, *op. cit.*, p. 15.
168. P. Irwin, *op. cit.*, p. 163.
169. J. Vansina, *The Children of Woot*, p. 227.
170. See for example C. Westermann, *Genesis*, pp. 74, 703; A. de Pury, 'Genèse XXXIV et l'histoire', *RB* 86 (1969), pp. 1-49; G.W. Coats, *Genesis*, ed. R. Knierim and G.M. Tucker (FOTL 1; Michigan, 1983), pp. 22f.
171. See W.H. Kelber, *The Oral and Written Gospel* (Philadelphia, 1983), pp. 13-24.
172. J. Vansina, *Oral Tradition as History* (London, 1985), p. 94.
173. C. Westermann, *Die Verheissungen*, pp. 34-38; *Genesis*, pp. 73-90.
174. J. Vansina, *op. cit.*, p. 172.
175. See pp. 84-85.
176. D.P. Henige, *op. cit.*, p. 11.
177. *Ibid.*, p. 190.
178. G. W Coats, 'Genesis', in *The Forms of the Old Testament Literature*, Vol. I, ed. R. Knierim and G.M. Tucker (Michigan, 1983), pp. 9-10.
179. R. Finnegan, *Oral Poetry* (Cambridge, 1979), p. 151.

BIBLIOGRAPHY

Aarne, A. and S. Thompson, *The Types of the Folktale: A Classification and Bibliography* (FF No. 184, 2nd edn rev.; Helsinki, 1964).
Abrahams, R.D., 'The Complex Relations in Simple Forms', *Genre* 2 (1969), pp. 104-28.
Ahlström, G.W., 'Oral and Written Transmission', *HTR* 59 (1966), pp. 69-81.
Albright, W.F., *From the Stone Age to Christianity* (2nd edn; New York, 1957).
Alt, A., 'Der Gott der Väter', in *Kleine Schriften zur Geschichte des Volkes Israel*, Vol. I (Munich, 1953), pp. 1-78.
Alter, R., *The Art of Biblical Narrative* (London, 1981).
Anderson, G.K. and R. Warnock, *Tradition and Revolt* (Illinois, 1967).
Anderson, G.W., 'Some Aspects of the Uppsala School of Old Testament Study', *HTR* 43 (1950), pp. 239-56.
Andersson, T.M., *The Problem of Icelandic Saga Origins* (London, 1964).
—*The Icelandic Family Saga: An Analytic Reading* (Cambridge, 1967).
—'The Icelandic Sagas', in *Heroic Epic and Saga*, ed. F.J. Onias (London, 1978), pp. 144-71.
Ashkenazi, T., 'Tribes semi-nomades de la Palestine du Nord', in *Etudes d'ethnographie, de sociologie et d'ethnologie* (Paris, 1938), pp. 187-210.
Baker, D.W., 'The Diversity and Unity in the Literary Structure of Genesis', in *Essays on the Patriarchal Narrative*, ed. A.R. Millard and D.J. Wiseman (Leicester, 1980), pp. 189-205.
Barnes, D.B., 'Toward the Establishment of Principles for the Study of Folklore and Literature' *SFQ* 43 (1979), pp. 5-16.
Barr, J., *Old and New in Interpretation* (London, 1966).
Barthes, R., 'La Lutte avec l'ange: analyse textuelle de Genèse 32:23-33', in *Analyse structurelle et exégèse biblique*, ed. R. Barthes and F. Bovon (Neuchatel, 1971), pp. 27-40.
Bartlett, F.C., *Remembering* (Cambridge, 1932).
—'Some Experiments of the Reproduction of Folk Stories', in *The Study of Folklore*, ed. A. Dundes (Englewood Cliffs, 1965), pp. 243-58.
Bartlett, J.R., 'The Land of Seir and the Brotherhood of Edom' *JTS* 20 (1969), pp. 1-20.
—'The Brotherhood of Edom', *JSOT* 4 (1977), pp. 2-27.
Barton, J., *Reading the Old Testament* (London, 1984).
Bascom, W.R., 'The Relationship of Yoruba Folklore to Divining', *JAF* 56 (1943), pp. 127-31.
—'Folklore and Anthropology', *JAF* 66 (1953), pp. 283-90.
—'Four Functions of Folklore', *JAF* 67 (1954), pp. 333-68.
—'Verbal Art', *JAF* 68 (1955), pp. 245-52.
—'The Forms of Folklore: Prose Narratives', *JAF* 78 (1954), pp. 3-20.
—*Ifa Divination: Communication between Gods and Men in West Africa* (Bloomington, 1969).
Bauml, F.H. and E. Spielmann, 'From Illiteracy to Literacy. Prolegomena to a Study of the Nibelungenlied', *Forum for Modern Language Studies* 10 (1974), pp. 248-59.

Bausinger, H., *Formen der Volkspoesie* (Berlin, 1980).
Beidelman, T.D., *W. Robertson-Smith and the Sociological Study of Religion* (London, 1974).
Ben-Amos, D., 'Analytical Categories and Ethnic Genres', *Genre* 2 (1969), pp. 275-301.
—'Toward a Definition of Folklore in Context', in *Toward New Perspectives in Folklore*, ed. A. Paredes and R. Bauman (Austin, 1972), pp. 3-15.
—ed., *Folklore Genres* (Austin, 1976).
—'Introduction: Folklore in African Society', in *Forms of Folklore in Africa*, ed. B. Lindfors (Texas, 1977), pp. 1-34.
—'The Modern Local Historian', *Folklore in the Modern World*, ed. R.M. Dorsen (London, 1978), pp. 327-43.
—'The Concept of Motif in Folklore', in *Folklore Studies in the Twentieth Century*, ed. V.J. Newall (1980), pp. 17-36.
Benson, L.D., 'The Literary Character of Anglo-Saxon Formulaic Poetry', *PMLA* 81 (1966), pp. 334-41.
Bentzen, A., *Introduction to the Old Testament*, 2 vols. (Copenhagen, 1952).
Berendsohn, W., 'Enfache Formen', *Handwörterbuch des deutschen Märchens*, ed. L. Mackenson (Berlin, 1930-33), Vol. I, pp. 484-98.
Biebuck, D.P., 'The African Heroic Epic', *Heroic Epic and Saga*, ed. F.J. Onias (London, 1978), pp. 336-68.
Birkeland, H., *Zum hebräischen Traditionswesen: Die Komposition der prophetischen Bücher des Alten Testaments* (Oslo, 1938).
Blake, N.F., 'The Dating of Old English Poetry', *An English Miscellany presented to W.S. Mackie*, ed. B.S. Lee (London, 1977), pp. 14-27.
Blau, J.L., ed., *Essays in Jewish Life and Thought* (New York, 1969).
Boas, F., 'Stylistic Aspects of Primitive Literature', *JAF* 38 (1925), pp. 329-39.
Bødker, L., ed., *Selected Papers on Folklore by C.W. von Sydow* (Copenhagen, 1948).
Bolte, J. and G. Polívka, *Anmerkungen zu den Kinder- und Hausmärchen der Brüder Grimm*, 5 vols. (Leipzig, 1913-1932).
Bowra, C.M., *The Meaning of a Heroic Age* (Newcastle, 1957).
Bremond, C., 'The Clandestine Ox: The Transformation of an African Tale', *NLH* 8 (1977), pp. 393-409.
Brewer, D., 'The Gospels and the Laws of Folktale', *Folklore* 90 (1979), pp. 37-52.
Bruford, A., 'Recitation or Re-creation? Examples from South Uist Storytelling', *Scottish Studies* 22 (1978), pp. 27-44.
Brueggemann, W., 'David and His Theologian', *CBQ* 30 (1968), pp. 156-81.
Bryce, G.E., 'Structuralism and History: The Structure of the Narrative in Myth, Folktale, and the Synoptic Gospels', *Scripture in History and Theology: Essays in Honor of J.C. Rylaarsdam*, ed. A.L. Merrill and T.W. Overholt (Pittsburgh, 1977), pp. 301-42.
Brynjulf, A., 'Category and Function', *Fabula* 10 (1969), pp. 63-69.
Buss, M.J., 'The Idea of Sitz im Leben—History and Critique', *ZAW* 96 (1978), pp. 157-70.
—ed., *Encounter with the Text* (Missoula, 1979).
Bynum, D.E., 'The Generic Nature of Oral Epic Poetry', *Genre* 2 (1969), pp. 236-357.
Caird, G.B., *The Language and Imagery of the Bible* (London, 1980).
Carlson, R.A., *David the Chosen King. A Traditio-Historical Approach to the Second Book of Samuel* (ET Stockholm, 1964).

Bibliography

Chadwick, H.M. and N.K., *The Growth of Literature*, 3 vols. (Cambridge, 1932-1940)
Chadwick, N.K., *The Heroic Age* (Cambridge, 1942).
Childs, B.S., *Memory and Tradition in Israel* (London, 1962).
—'Deuteronomic Formulae of the Exodus Tradition', *Hebräische Wortforschung*, Festschrift W. Baumgartner; SVT 16 (1967), pp. 30-39.
—'The Exegetical Significance of Canon for the Study of the Old Testament', *VTS* 29 (1977), pp. 66-80.
—*Introduction to the Old Testament as Scripture* (London, 1979).
Clark, W.M., 'The Patriarchal Traditions: The Biblical Tradition', *Israelite and Judean History*, ed. J.H. Hayes and J.M. Miller (Philadelphia, 1977).
Clements, R., *Abraham and David* (London, 1967).
Cohn, R.L., 'Narrative Structure and Canonical Perspective in Genesis', *JSOT* 25 (1983), pp. 3-16.
Conroy, C., 'Hebrew Epic: Historical Notes and Critical Reflections', *Biblica* 61 (1980), pp. 1-30.
Cook, S.A., 'Some Tendencies in Old Testament Criticism', *JTS* 26 (1925), pp. 156-73.
Coppens, J., 'La Bénédiction de Jacob. Son cadre historique à la lumière des parallèles ougaritiques', *SVT* (1957), pp. 97-115.
Crenshaw, J., *Gerhard von Rad* (Waco, 1978).
Cross, F.M., Jr, 'Yahweh and the God of the Patriarchs' *HTR* 55 (1962), pp. 225-59.
—*Canaanite Myth and Hebrew Epic* (Harvard, 1973).
Culley, R.C., 'An Approach to the Problem of Oral Tradition', *VT* 13 (1963), pp. 113-25.
—*Oral Formulaic Language in the Biblical Psalms* (Toronto, 1967).
—'Oral Tradition and Historicity', in *Studies in the Ancient Palestinian World*, ed. J. Wevers and D. Redford (Toronoto, 1972), pp. 102-16.
—*Studies in the Structure of Hebrew Narrative* (Missoula, 1976).
Danell, G.A., *Studies in the Name Israel in the Old Testament* (Uppsala, 1946).
Danielson, L., 'Toward the Analysis of Vernacular Texts: The Supernatural Narrative in Oral and Popular Print Sources', *JFI* 16 (1979), pp. 130-50.
Davenport, W.H., 'Marshallese Folklore Types', *JAF* 66 (1953), pp. 219-37.
Dégh, L., 'The Systematic Ordering of the Hungarian Legends', *International Society for Folk Narrative Research* (Antwerp, 1963), pp. 66-74.
—ed., *Folktales of Hungary* (Chicago, 1965).
—*Folktales and Society: Telling in a Hungarian Peasant Community* (Indiana, 1969).
Dégh, L., A. Vazsonyi, 'The Memorate and the Proto-Memorate', *JAF* 87 (1974), pp. 225-39.
—'Grimm's Household Tales and its Place in the Household: The Social Relevance of a Controversial Classic', *Western Folklore* 38 (1979), pp. 83-103.
Diedrich, F., *Die Anspielungen auf die Jakob-Tradition in Hosea 12,1—13,3* (Würzburg, 1977).
Doll, H.D., *Oral Interpretation of Literature* (London, 1982).
Dollerup, C., I. Reventlow and C. Rosenberg Hansen, 'A Case Study of Editorial Filters in Folktales: A Discussion of the Allerleirauh Tales in Grimm', *Fabula* 27 (1986), pp. 11-30.
Dorsson, R.M., 'Oral Tradition and Written History: The Case for the United States', *JFI* 1 (1964), pp. 220-30.
—'The Debate over the Trustworthiness of Oral Tradition History', *Volksüberlieferung*, Festschrift für Kurt Ranke (Göttingen, 1968), pp. 19-25.

—*The British Folklorist* (London, 1968).
—*African Folklore* (London, 1972).
—*Folklore and Fakelore: Essays Toward a Discipline Folklore Studies* (London, 1976).
—ed., *Folklore in the Modern World* (Paris, 1978).
Driver, S.R., *The Book of Genesis* (Westminster Commentaries; 9th edn; London, 1913).
Duffield, M.R., 'Some Thoughts on the Social Structures of Myth', *Approaches to Oral Tradition*, ed. R. Thelwall (Ulster, 1978), pp. 1-23.
Duggan, J.J., ed., *Oral Literature: Seven Essays* (London, 1975).
Dundes, A., *The Morphology of North American Indian Folktales* (FLC 195; Helsinki, 1964).
—'Text, Texture and Context', *SFQ* 28 (1964), pp. 251-65.
—*The Study of Folklore* (Englewood Cliffs, 1965).
—The Devolutionary Premise in Folklore Theory', *JFI* 6 (1969), pp. 5-19.
—*Analytic Essays in Folklore* (The Hague, 1975).
—*Varia Folklorica* (The Hague, 1978).
Duprée, L., 'The Retreat of the British Army from Kabul to Jalalabad in 1842: History and Folklore', *JFI* 4 (1967), pp. 50-74.
Edmonson, M.S., *Lore: An Introduction to the Science of Folklore and Literature* (New York, 1971).
Edwards, C.L. 'The Parry-Lord Theory meets Operational Structuralism', *JAF* 96 (1983), pp. 151-69.
Eissfeldt, O., *Hexateuch-Synopse* (Leipzig, 1922).
—'Stammessage und Novelle in den Geschichten von Jakob und von seinen Söhnen', in *Eucharisterion*, Gunkel-Festschrift, Vol. I (Göttingen, 1923), pp. 56-77.
—'Genesis', in *The Interpeter's Dictionary of the Bible*, Vol. II (New York, 1962), pp. 366-80.
—'Achronische, anachronische und synchronische Elemente in der Genesis', in Jaarbericht van het Vooraziatischegyptisch Genootschap, *Ex Oriente Lux* 17 (1963), pp. 161f.
—*Einleitung in das Alte Testament* (3rd edn; Tübingen, 1964).
Ellis, J.M., *One Fairy Story Too Many* (London, 1983).
Ellis, P.F., *The Yahwist: The Bible's First Theologian* (London, 1969).
—'The Origin of the Promises to the Patriarchs in the Older Sources of the Book of Genesis', *VT* 32 (1982), pp. 14-32.
Engnell, I., 'Methodological Aspects of Old Testament Study', *VTS* 7 (1960), pp. 13-30.
—*Critical Essays on the Old Testament* (ET London, 1970).
Ewald, H.A., *The History of Israel*, Vol. I (ET London, 1869).
Finnegan, R., *Limba Stores and Story Telling* (Oxford, 1967).
—*Oral Literature in Africa* (Oxford, 1970).
—'A Note on Oral Traidtion and Historical Evidence', *History and Theory* 9 (1970), pp. 193-201.
—'What is Oral Literature Anyway?', *Oral Literature and the Formula*, ed. B. Stolz and R. Shannon (Michigan, 1976), pp. 127-62.
—*Oral Poetry* (Oxford, 1977).
Fishbane, M., 'Composition and Structure in the Jacob Cycle (Gen. 25.19-35.22)', *JJS* 26 (1975), pp. 15-38.
Fohrer, G., *Introduction to the Old Testament* (ET New York, 1968).
Fokkelman, J.P., *Narrative Art in Genesis* (Amsterdam, 1975).

Foley, J.M. *Oral Traditional Literature. A Festschrift for A.B. Lord* (Ohio, 1981).
—*Oral Formulaic Theory and Research. An Introduction and Annotated Bibliography* (London, 1985).
Frazer, J.G., *Folk-lore in the Old Testament* (London, 1918).
—*Appollodorus* (London, 1921).
Fretheim, T.E., 'The Jacob Traditions. Theology and Hermeneutic', *Int* 26 (1972), pp. 419-36.
Frye, N., *Anatomy of Criticism: Four Essays* (Princeton, 1957).
Gammie, D.G., 'Theological Interpretation by Way of Literary and Tradition Analysis: Genesis 25-36', in *Encounter with the Text*, ed. M.J. Buss (Missoula, 1979), pp. 117-34.
de Geus, C.H., *The Tribes of Israel* (Amsterdam, 1976).
Geyer, J.B., 'The Joseph and Moses Narratives: Folktale and History', *JSOT* 15 (1980), pp. 51-56.
Gibert, P., 'Légende ou Saga?', *VT* 24 (1974), pp. 411-20.
—*Une Théorie de la légende* (Paris, 1979).
Goff, B.S., 'The Lost Yahwistic Account of the Conquest of Canaan', *JBL* 53 (1934), pp. 241-49.
Golka, F.W., 'The Aetiologies in the Old Testament', *JBL* 80 (1961), pp. 339-47.
Gomme, G.L., 'The Science of Folklore', *Folk-lore Journal* 3 (1885), pp. 1-16.
—*Folklore as an Historical Science* (London, 1908).
Goody, J., *The Domestication of the Savage Mind* (London, 1977).
Grambo, R., 'The Conceptions of Variant and Motif: A Theoretical Approach', *Fabula* 16 (1976), pp. 243-56.
Gray, B., 'Repetition in Oral Literature', *JAF* 84 (1971), pp. 289-303.
Gressmann, H., 'Mythen und Mythologie', *RGG* (1913), cols. 618-22.
—'Sage und Geschichte in den Patriarchenerzählungen', *ZAW* 30 (1910), pp. 1-34.
Grimm, J.L.L. and W.C., *Kinder- und Hausmärchen*, 2 vols. (Berlin, 1812 and 1815; 2nd edn, 3 vols. 1819 and 1822); ET, M. Hunt, *Grimm's Household Tales* (London, 1892).
—*Deutsche Sagen*, 2 vols. (Berlin, 1816 and 1818).
—*Deutsche Mythologie* (Berlin, 1835; 4th edn, vol. II, 1876); ET, J.S. Stallybrass, *Teutonic Mythology*, vols. I-IV (London, 1883-1885).
Grobman, N.R., 'A Schema for the Study of the Sources and Literary Simulations of Folkloric Phenomena', *SFQ* (1979), pp. 17-37.
Groome, F.H., ed., *Gypsy Folktales* (Pennsylvania, 1963).
Gross, W., 'Jakob, der Mann des Sagens. Zur Traditionsgeschichte und Theologie der priesterschriftlichen Jakobsüberlieferung', *Bib* 49 (1968), pp. 321-44.
Gunkel, H., *Schöpfung und Chaos in Urzeit und Endzeit* (Göttingen, 1895).
—*Genesis übersetzt und erklärt* (Göttingen, 1901, ET of Intro., *The Legends of Genesis*, [New York, 1964]; 3rd edn, Göttingen, 1910).
—'Die israelitische Literatur', in *Die Kultur der Gegenwart*, I, ed. P. Hinneberg (Berlin, 1906), pp. 51-102.
—'Jakob', *Preussische Jahrbücher* 176 (1919), pp. 339-62.
—*Das Märchen im Alten Testament* (Tübingen, 1921); ET, The Folktale in the Old Testament (Sheffield, 1987).
—'Sagen und Legenden', *RGG* (1931), cols. 49-60.
Gunn, D.M., 'The Battle Report and Scribal Convention', *JBL* 93 (1974), pp. 513-18.
—*The Story of King David: Genre and Interpretation* (JSOT Supplements, 6; Sheffield, 1978).

Guttgemanns, E., 'Fundamentals of a Grammar of Oral Literature', *Patterns in Oral Literature*, ed. H. Jason and E. Segal (Chicago, 1977), pp. 77-97.
Hahn, H.F., 'Wellhausen's Interpretation of Israel's Religious History', in *Essays in Jewish Life and Thought*, ed. J.L. Blau (New York, 1959), pp. 299-308.
Hals, R.M., 'Legend: A Case Study in Old Testament Form Critical Terminology', *CBQ* 34 (2972), pp. 166-76.
Hand, W.D., 'The Status of European and American Legend Studies', *Current Anthropology* 6 (1965), pp. 439-65.
Hansen, W.F., 'The Homeric Epics and Oral Poetry', *Heroic Epics and Saga*, ed. F.J. Onias (London, 1978), pp. 7-26.
Hayes, J.H. and J.M. Miller, *Israelite and Judean History* (Philadelphia, 1977).
Hayes, J.H., *Old Testament Form Criticism* (Trinity, 1974).
—*An Introduction to Old Testament Study* (Nashville, 1979).
Henige, D.P., 'Oral Tradition and Chronology', *Journal of African History* 12 (1971), pp. 371-89.
—*The Chronology of Oral Tradition* (Oxford, 11974).
Herion, G.A., 'The Role of Historical Narrative in Biblical Thought: The Tendencies Underlying Old Testament Historiography', *JSOT* 21 (1981), pp. 25-57.
Hermisson, H.J., 'Jakobs Kampf am Jabbok (Gen. 32:23-33)', *ZThK* 71 (1974), pp. 239-61.
Herskovits, M.J. and F.S., *Dahomean Narrative: A Cross-Cultural Analysis* (Evanston, Ill., 1958).
Hillers, D.R., 'Critical Note: *Pahad Yishaq*', *JBL* 91 (1972), pp. 90-92.
Hoftijzer, J., *Die Verheissungen an die drei Erzväter* (Leiden, 1956).
—'David and the Tekoite Woman', *VT* 20 (1970), pp. 419-44.
Innes, G., *Kaabu and Faludu: Historical Narratives of the Gambian Mandinka* (London, 1976).
—*Kelefa Saane, His Career Recounted by two Mandinka Bards* (London, 1978).
Irvin, D., *Mytharion: The Comparison of Tales from the Old Testament and the Ancient Near East* (Neukirchen, 1978).
Irwin, P., *Liptako Speaks: History from Oral Tradition in Africa* (Princeton, 1981).
Jabbour, A., 'Memorial Transmission in Old English Poetry', *Chaucer Review* 3 (1969), pp 174-90.
Jacobs, M., 'A Look Ahead in Oral Literature Research', *JAF* 79 (1966), pp. 413-27.
James, W., *Kwanim Pa: The Making of the Urduk People* (Oxford, 1979).
Jason, H., 'A Model for Narrative Structure in Oral Literature', *Patterns of Oral Literature*, ed. H. Jason and D. Segal (Chicago, 1977), pp. 99-139.
—*Ethnopoetry* (Bonn, 1977).
—'Content Analysis of Oral Literature: A Discussion', *Patterns in Oral Literature*, ed. H. Jason and D. Segal (Chicago, 1977), pp. 261-310.
Jason, H. and Segal D., eds., *Patterns in Oral Literature* (Chicago, 1977).
Jason, H., 'Aspects of the Fabulous in Oral Literature', *Fabula* 19 (1978), pp. 14-31.
—'The Story of David and Goliath: A Folk Epic?', *Biblica* 60 (1979), pp. 36-70.
Jason, H. and A. Kempinski, 'How Old are Folktales?', *Fabula* 22 (1981), pp. 1-27.
Jenks, A.W., *The Elohist North Israelite Tradition* (Missoula, 1977).
Jolles, A., *Einfache Formen* (Halle, 1929, reprinted Tübingen, 1964).
Kelber, W.H., *The Oral and Written Gospel* (Philadelphia, 1983).
Kellogg, R., 'Oral Literature', *NLH* 4 (1973), pp. 55-66.
—'Oral Narrative, Written Books', *Genre* 10 (1977), pp. 655-65.
—'Literature, Nonliterature and Oral Tradition', *NLH* 8 (1977), pp. 531-34.

Kevers, P., 'Étude Littéraire de Genèse, XXIV', *RB* 87 (1980), pp. 38-86.
Kitteridge, G.L., *Francis James Child's English and Scottish Popular Ballads* (Boston, 1932).
Kirk, G.S., *Homer and the Oral Tradition* (London, 1976).
—*Myth* (Cambridge, 1970).
Klatt, W., *Hermann Gunkel: zu seiner Theologie der Religionsgeschichte und zur Entstehung der formesgeschichtlichen Methode* (Göttingen, 1969).
Knight, D.H., *Rediscovering the Traditions of Israel* (SBL Dissertations 9; Missoula, 1973).
—'Wellhausen and the Interpretation of Israel's Literature', *Semeia* 25 (1982), pp. 21-36.
Knierim, R., 'Old Testament Form Criticism Reconsidered', *Int* 27 (1973), pp. 435-68.
Koch, K., *Was ist Formgeschichte?* (Neukirchen, 1964); ET *The Growth of the Biblical Tradition* (London, 1969).
Krappe, A.H., *Études de mythologie et de folklore germaniques* (Paris, 1928).
Kroëber, K., 'Scarface vs. Scar-face: The Problem of Versions', *JFI* 18 (1981), pp. 99-124.
—ed., *Traditional Literatures of the American Indian* (London, 1981).
Krohn, K., *Folklore Methodology* (ET Austin, 1971).
Labrie-Bouthillier, V., 'Les Expériences sur la transmission orale: d'un modèle individuel à un modèle collectif', *Fabula* 17 (1977), pp. 1-17.
Leache, M. and Fried, J., *Funk and Wagnall's Standard Dictionary of Folklore, Mythology and Legend* (New York, 1949).
Lemche, N.P. 'The Greek "Amphictyony"—Could it be a Prototype for the Israelite Society in the Period of the Judges?', *JSOT* 4 (1977), pp. 48-59.
Lindfors, B., ed., *Forms of Folklore in Africa* (London, 1977).
Lindow, J., 'A Note on the Sources of Redundancy in Oral Epic', *JAF* 87 (1974), pp. 365-69.
Littleton, C.S., 'A Two Dimensional Schema for the Classification of Narratives', *JAF* 78 (1965), pp. 21-27.
Littman, E., *Arabische Beduinenerzählungen* (Strassburg, 1908).
Ljung, I., *Tradition and Interpretation* (Uppsala, 1978).
Lloyd-Jones, H., Pearl, V., and Worden, B., eds., *History and Imagination* (London, 1981).
Lloyd-Jones, H., 'Remarks on the Homeric Question', *History and Imagination*, ed. H. Lloyd-Jones, V. Pearl, and B. Worden (London, 1981), pp. 15-29.
Loewenstamm, S.E., 'The Divine Grants of Land to the Patriarchs', *JAOS* 91 (1971), pp. 509f.
Lowie, R.H., 'Oral Tradition and History', *JAF* 30 (1917), pp. 161-67.
Long, B.O., *The Problems of Etiological Narrative in the Old Testament* (Berlin, 1968).
—'Recent Field Studies in Oral Literature and their Bearing on Old Testament Criticism', *VT* 24 (1974), pp. 187-98.
Lo Nigro, S., 'Tradition et style du conte populaire', *Internationaler Kongress der Volkserzählungsforschung in Kiel und Kopenhagen*, ed. K. Ranke (Berlin, 1961), pp. 152-60.
Lord, A.B., *The Singer of Tales* (New York 1960).
—'A Comparative Analysis', in *Embundu Folktales from Angola*, compiled and translated by M. Ennis (Boston, 1962).
—'Yugoslav Epic Folk Poetry', in *The Study of Folklore*, ed. A. Dundes (Englewood Cliffs,

1965), pp. 265-69.
—'Perspectives on Recent Work on Oral Literature', in *Oral Literature: Seven Essays*, ed. J.J. Duggan (London, 1975), pp. 1-24.
—'The Gospels as Oral Traditional Literature', in *The Relationship among the Gospels*, ed. W.O. Walker (San Antonio, 1978), pp. 31-91.
—'Memory, Fixity and Genre', in *Oral Traditional Poetries in Oral Traditional Literature: A Festschrift for A.B. Lord*, ed. J.M. Foley (Ohio, 1981), pp. 451-61.
Lowie, R.H., 'Some Cases of Repeated Reproduction', in *The Study of Folklore*, ed. A. Dundes (Englewood Cliffs, 1965), pp. 259-65.
Luthi, M., 'Urform und Zielform in Sage und Märchen', *Fabula* 10 (1969), pp. 41-54.
—'Aspects of the Märchen and the Legend', *Genre* 2 (1969), pp. 162-78.
Maranda, K.E., 'The Concept of Folklore', *Midwest Folklore* 13 (1963), pp. 69-88.
Martin-Achard, R., 'Un exégète devant Genèse 32:23-33', *Analyse structural et exégèse biblique* (Neuchatel, 1971), pp. 41-62.
McKane, W., *Studies in the Patriarchal Narratives* (Edinburgh, 1979).
McLuhan, M., *The Gutenberg Galaxy* (London, 1962).
—*Understanding the Media. The Extensions of Man* (London, 1967).
McMillan, D.J., 'A Survey of Theories Concerning the Oral Transmission of the Traditional Ballad', *SFQ* 28 (1964), pp. 299-309.
Melchin, K.R., 'Literary Sources in the Joseph Story', *Science et Esprit* 31 (1979), pp. 93-101.
Merrill, A.L. and Overholt, T.W., eds., *Scripture in History and Theology: Essays in Honor of J.C. Rylaarsdam* (Pittsburgh, 1977).
Michaelis-Jena, R., 'Oral Tradition and the Brothers Grimm', *Folklore* 82 (1971), pp. 265-75.
Millar, R.W., 'Oral Poetry and Dumuzi's Dream', *Scripture in Context*, ed. C.D. Evans, W.W. Hallo, and J.B. White (Pittsburgh, 1980), pp. 27-58.
—'Methods of Studying the Patriarchal Narratives as Ancient Texts', *Essays on the Patriarchal Narratives*, ed. A.R. Millard and D.J. Wiseman (Leicester, 1980), pp. 43-58.
Millard, A.R. and D.J. Wiseman, ed., *Essays on the Patriarchal Narratives* (Leicester, 1980).
Miller, J.C., *Kings and Kinsmen* (Oxford, 1976).
Miscall, P.D., 'The Jacob and Joseph Stories as Analogies', *JSOT* (1978), pp. 28-40.
Mitchell, J.G., 'A Study of the Jacob Tradition in the Old Testament', *Dis. Ab.* 31 (1970/71), pp. 457-58.
Moore, J.R., 'The Influence of Transmission on the English Ballad', *Modern Language Review* 11 (1916), pp. 385-408.
Moser-Rath, E., 'Literature and Folk Tradition: Sources for Folk Narrative of the Seventeenth Centuries', *JFI* 5 (1968), pp. 175-87.
Muilenburg, J., 'Form Criticism and Beyond', *JBL* 88 (1969), pp. 1-18.
Murtonen, A., 'The Fixation in Writing of Various Parts of the Pentateuch', *VT* 3 (1953), pp. 46-53.
Newall, V.J., *Folklore Studies in the Twentieth Century* (Suffolk, 1980).
Nicoholson, E.W., *Exodus and Sinai in History and Tradition* (London, 1973).
Nielson, E., *Oral Tradition* (London, 1954).
Noth, M., *Überlieferungsgeschichte des Pentateuch* (Stuttgart, 1948).
—*Das System der zwölf Stämme Israels* (BWANT 4/1; Stuttgart, 1930).
—*Die Geschichte Israels* (3rd edn; Göttingen, 1956).
North, C.R., 'Oral Tradition and Written Documents', *ExpT* 66 (1954/55), pp. 39ff.

—'The Place of Oral Tradition in the Growth of the Old Testament', *ExpT* 61 (1949/50), pp. 292-96.
Nutt, A., 'History, Tradition and Historic Myth', *Folklore* 12 (1901), pp. 336-39.
Nyberg, H.S., 'Das Textkritische demonstriert', *ZAW* 52 (1934), pp. 242-46.
—*Die Religionen des Alten Iran* (German translation; Leipzig, 1938).
Olrik, A., 'Epische Gesetze der Volksdichtung', *Zeitschrift für Deutsches Altertum und Deutsche Literatur*, 51 (1909), pp. 1-12; ET, *The Study of Folklore*, ed. A. Dundes (Englewood Cliffs, 1965), pp. 129-41.
Ong, W.J., 'Oral Remembering and Narrative Structures', in *Georgetown University Round Table on Languages and Linguistics, 1981* (Washington, 1982).
—*Orality and Literature* (London, 1982).
Oinas, F.J., ed., *Heroic Epic and Saga* (London, 1978).
O'Nolan, K., 'Formula in Oral Tradition', in *Approaches to Oral Tradition*, ed. R. Thelwall (Ulster, 1978), pp. 24-34.
Opland, J., '"Scoop" and "Imbongi" Anglo-Saxon and Bantu Oral Poets', *English Studies in Africa* 14 (1971), pp. 161-78.
—'Imbong Nezibongo: The Xhosa Tribal Poet and the Contemporary Poetic Tradition', *PMLA* 90 (1975), pp. 185-208.
—*Anglo-Saxon Oral Poetry* (Michigan, 1980).
Oring, E., 'The Devolutionary Premiss: A Definitional Delusion?', *Western Folklore* 12 (1975), pp. 36-44.
—'Transmission and Degeneration', *Fabula* 19 (1978), pp. 193-210.
Ortutay, G., 'Principles of Oral Transmission in Folk Culture', *Acta Ethnographica* 8 (1959), pp. 175-221.
—'Principles of Oral Transmission in Folk Culture', pp. 132-73, and 'Jacob Grimm and Folklore Study in Hungary', pp. 182-202, in *Hungarian Folklore Essays*, ed. G. Ortutay (Budapest, 1957).
Pentikäinen, J., 'Repertoire Analysis', in *Folk Narrative Research: Some Papers Presented at the VI Congress of the International Society of Folk Narrative Research*, ed. J. Pentikäinen (Helsinki, 1976).
—*Oral Repertoire and World View* (Helsinki, 1978).
—'Oral Transmission of Knowledge', in *Folklore in the Modern World*, ed. R.M. Dorson (Paris, 1978), pp. 237-52.
Perlitt, L., *Vatke und Wellhausen* (Berlin, 1965).
Pfeiffer, R.H., 'A Non-Israelite Source of the Book of Genesis', *ZAW* 48 (1930), pp. 66-73.
Polzin, R.M. and Rothman, E., eds., *The Biblical Mosaic* (Philadelphia, 1982).
Porter, J.R., 'Pre-Islamic Arabic Historical Traditions and the Early Historical Narratives of the Old Testament', *JBL* 87 (1968), pp. 17-26.
Proff, V., *Morphology of the Folktale* (ET 2nd edn, revised; Austin, 1968).
—'Structure and History in the Study of the Fairy Tale', ET in *Semeia* 11 (1978), pp. 57-83.
de Pury, A., *Promesse divine et légende cultuelle dans le cycle de Jacob: Genèse 28 et les traditions patriarcales* (Paris, 1975).
—'Genèse XXXIV et l'histoire', *RB* 74 (1969), pp. 5-49.
Rad, G. von, *Das formgeschichtliche Problem des Hexateuch* (BWANT 4/26; Stuttgart, 1926) reprinted in *Gesammelte Studien* (München, 1958), pp. 9-86; ET *The Problem of the Hexateuch and Other Essays* (Edinburgh, 1966).
—*Theologie des Alten Testaments*, I (München, 1957).
—*Das erste Buch Mose, Genesis* (Göttingen, 1972); ET *Genesis* (OTL; London, 1972).

Ranke, K., 'Einfache Formen', *JFI* 4 (1967), pp. 17-31.
Rendtorff, R., *Das überlieferungsgeschichtliche Problem des Pentateuch* (BZAW, 47; Berlin, 1977).
Richter, W., 'Formgeschichte und Sprachwissenschaft', *ZAW* 82 (1970), pp. 216-25.
—*Exegese als Literaturwissenschaft* (Göttingen, 1972).
Rinngren, H., *Israelite History* (ET Philadelphia, 1966).
—'Oral and Written Transmission in the Old Testament', *Studia Theologica* 3 (1949), pp. 35-59.
Rogerson, J.W., 'The Hebrew Conception of Corporate Personality: A Re-examination', *JTS* 21 (1970), pp. 11-16.
—*Myth in Old Testament Interpretation* (BZAW, 134; Berlin, 1974).
—*Anthropology and the Old Testament* (Oxford, 1978).
Rölleke, H., ed., *Die älteste Märchensammlung der Brüder Grimm* (Collogny-Genève, 1975).
—'Allerleirauh. Eine bisher unbekannte Fassung vor Grimm', *Fabula* 13 (1972), pp. 153-59.
Rose, M., 'Entmilitarisierung des Kriegs?', *Erwägungen zu den Patriarchen-Erzählungen des Genesis* (BZAW 49; Berlin, 1979), pp. 197-211.
Rose, M., 'Yahweh in Israel—Quos in Edom?', *JSOT* 4 (1977), pp. 28-34.
Roth, W., 'The Text is the Medium: An Interpretation of the Jacob Stories in Genesis', *Encounter with the Text*, ed. M.J. Buss (Missoula, 1979), pp. 103-17.
Rowley, H.H., ed., *The Old Testament and Modern Study, A Generation of Discovery and Research* (Oxford, 1951).
Scheub, H., 'The Technique of the Expansible Image in Xhosa Ntsomi-Performances" in *Forms of Folklore in Africa*, ed. B. Lindfors (London, 1977), pp. 37-63.
—'Oral Narrative Process and the Use of Models', in *Varia Folklorica*, ed. A. Dundes (The Hague, 1978), pp. 353-77.
Schmid, H.H., *Der sogenannte Jahwist* (Zürich, 1976).
Schmidt, F.W., 'Die Volkssage als Kuntswerk', *Niederdeutsche Zeitschrift in Volkskunde* 7 (1929), pp. 129-45, 230-44. Reprinted in *Vergleichende Sagenforschung*, ed. L. Petzoldt (Darmstadt, 1969), pp. 21-65.
Schwartz, E., 'The Problem of Literary Genres', *Criticism* 13 (1971), pp. 113-30.
Shils, E., *Tradition* (London, 1981).
Simpson, C.A., *The Early Traditions of Israel. A Critical Analysis of the Predeuteronomic Narrative of the Hexateuch* (Oxford, 1948).
Skinner, J., *Genesis* (ICC; Edinburgh, 1910).
Smend, R., *Die Erzählung des Hexateuch auf ihre Quellen untersucht* (Berlin, 1912).
Smith, M., 'The Present State of Old Testament Studies', *JBL* 88 (1969), pp. 19-35.
Solheim, S., 'Historical Legend—Historical Function', *Acta Ethnographica* 19 (1970), pp. 341-46.
Speiser, E.A., 'I Know Not the Day of My Death', *JBL* 74 (1955), pp. 252-56.
—*Genesis* (Anchor Bible; 3rd edn; New York, 1981).
Stahl, S.K.D., 'The Oral Personal Narrative in its Generic Context', *Fabula* 18 (1977), pp. 18-39.
—'Strife in Oral and Written Narratives', *SFQ* 43 (1979), pp 39-62.
—'Narrative Genres: A Question of Academic Assumptions' *Fabula* 21 (1980), pp. 82-87.
Strus, A., 'Etymologies des noms propres dans Gen. 29:32–30:24. Valeurs littéraires et fonctionnelles', *Salesianum* 40 (1978), pp. 57-72.
Sydow, C.W. von, 'Kategorien der Prosa-Volksdichtung' and 'Popular Prose Traditions and their Classification', in *Selected Papers on Folklore* (Copenhagen, 1978), pp. 60-85, 127-44.

Bibliography 149

Talbert, C.H., 'Oral and Independent or Literary and Interdependent: A Response to A.B. Lord', *The Relationship among the Gospels*, ed. W.O. Walker (San Antonio, 1978), pp. 93-102.
Talmon, S., 'The Comparative Method in Biblical Interpretation. Principles and Problems', *VTS* 29 (1978), pp. 320-56.
Tannen, D., 'Oral and Literate Strategies in Spoken and Written Narratives', *Language* 58 (1982), pp. 1-21.
—ed., *Spoken and Written Language: Exploring Orality and Literacy* (Englewood Cliffs, 1982).
Taylor, A., 'A Theory of Indo-European Märchen', *JAF* 44 (1931), pp. 54-60.
—'Folklore and the Student of Literature', in *The Study of Folklore*, ed. A. Dundes (New Jersey, 1965), pp. 34-42.
Tedlock, D., 'Toward an Oral Poetics', *NLH* 8 (1977), pp. 507-17.
—'The Spoken Word and the Work of Interpretation in American Indian Religion', ed. K. Kroeber (London, 1981), pp. 15-59.
Thelwall, R., ed., *Approaches to Oral Tradition* (Ulster, 1978).
Thoms, W., 'Folklore', in *The Study of Folklore*, ed. A. Dundes (Englewood Cliffs, 1965), pp. 4-6.
Thompson, M.E.W., *Situation and Theology. Old Testament Interpretation of the Syro-Ephraimite War* (Sheffield, 1982).
Thompson, R.J., *Moses in the Law in a Century of Criticism since Graf*, SUT 19 (Leiden, 1970).
Thompson, S., *The Folktale* (New York, 1946).
—'Folklore at Midcentury', *Midwest Folklore* 1 (1951), pp. 5-12.
—*Motif-Index of Folk Literature*, 6 vols. (Bloomington, 1955-1958).
Thompson, T.L., *The Historicity of the Patriarchal Narratives: The Quest for the Historical Abraham* (BZAW, 133; Berlin, 1974).
—'Conflict Themes in the Jacob Narratives', *Semeia* 15 (1979), pp. 5-26.
—'History and Tradition: A Response to J.B. Geyer', *JSOT* 15 (1980, pp. 57-61.
Tillhagen, C.H., 'Was ist eine Sage?', *Acta Ethnographica* 13 (1964), pp. 9-17.
Todorov, T., 'The Origin of Genres', *NLH* 8 (1974), pp. 159-70.
—*Les Genres du discours* (Paris, 1978).
Tucker, G.M., *Form Criticism of the Old Testament* (Philadelphia, 1971).
Utley, F.L., 'The Study of Folk Literature: Its Scope and Use', *JAF* 71 (1958), pp. 139-48.
—'Folk Literature: An Operational Definition', in *The Study of Folklore*, ed. A. Dundes (Englewood Cliffs, 1965), pp. 7-24.
—'Oral Genres as Bridge to Written Literature', *Genre* 2 (1969), pp. 91-103.
Van Seters, J., *Abraham in History and Tradition* (New Haven and London, 1975).
—'Confessional Reformulation in the Exilic Period', *VT* 22 (1972), pp. 448-59.
—'Tradition and Social Change in Ancient Israel', *Perspectives in Religious Studies* 7 (1980), pp. 96-113.
—'The Religion of the Patriarchs in Genesis', *Biblica* 61 (1980), pp. 229-33.
—'Histories and Historians of the Ancient Near East: The Israelites', *Orientalia* 50 (1981), pp. 137-85.
—*In Search of History* (London, 1983).
Vansina, J., *Oral Tradition* (ET, London, 1973).
—'Comment: Traditions of Genesis', *Journal of African History* 15 (1974), pp. 317-22.
—*The Children of Woot: A History of the Kuba Peoples* (Folkestone, 1978).
—*Oral Tradition as History* (London, 1983).

Vaux, R. de, *Histoire ancienne d'Israël*, Vol. I (Paris, 1971), Vol. II (Paris, 1973).
Voigt, V., 'Some Problems of Narrative Structure Universals in Folklore', *Acta Ethnographica* 21 (1972), pp. 57-72.
—'Towards a Theory of Genres in Folklore', in *Folklore Today*, ed. L. Dégh, H. Glassie, and F. Onias (Bloomington, 1976), pp. 485-96.
Wagner, N.E., 'Pentateuchal Criticism: No Clear Future', *CTJ* 13 (1967), pp. 225-32.
Walker, W.O., ed., *The Relationship among the Gospels* (San Antonio, 1978).
Ward, D., 'The Performance and Perception of Folklore and Literature', *Fabula* 20 (1979), pp. 256-64.
Ward, J.M. 'The Message of the Prophet Hosea', *Int* 23 (1969), pp. 387-407.
Warner, S.M., 'Primitive Saga Men', *VT* 29 (1979), pp. 325-35.
Warszawa, J.K., 'Legend in Literature and Folklore', *Fabula* 10 (1969), pp. 111-17.
Weimar, P., 'Aufbau und Struktur der priesterschriftlichen Jakobsgeschichte', *ZAW* 86 (1974), pp. 174-203.
Weiser, *The Old Testament: Its Formation and Development* (New York, 1961).
Wellhausen, J., 'Die Composition des Hexateuchs', *Jahrbücher für Deutsche Theologie* 21 (1876), pp. 392-450, 531-602; 22 (1877), pp. 407-79.
—*Prolegomena zur Geschichte Israels* (Berlin, 1883; 3rd edn, 1886); ET *Prolegomena to the History of Israel* (Edinburgh, 1885).
Westermann, C., *Die Verheissungen an die Väter* (Göttingen, 1976).
—*Genesis* (BKAT; Neukirchen, 1981); ET *Genesis 12-36: A Commentary* (London, 1986).
Whallon, W., *Formula, Character and Content. Studies in Homeric, Old English and Old Testament Poetry* (Cambridge, Mass., 1969).
—'Biblical Poetry and Homeric Epic', in *Parnassus Revisited*, ed. A.C. Yu (Chicago, 1973), pp. 214-20.
Widengren, G., *Literary and Psychological Aspects of the Hebrew Prophets* (Uppsala, 1948).
—Oral Tradition and Written Literature among the Hebrews in the Light of Arabic Evidence with Special Regard to Prose Narratives', *Acta Orientalia* 23 (1959), pp. 201-62.
—'Myth and History in Israelite Jewish Thought', *Culture in History*, ed. S. Diamond (New York, 1960), pp. 467-95.
Wilgus, D.K., 'The Text is the Thing', *JAF* 86 (1973), pp. 241-52.
Willis, J.T., 'Ivan Engnell's Contribution to Old Testament Scholarship', *ThZ* 26 (1970), pp. 385-94.
Wilson, R.R., *Genealogy and History in the Biblical World* (London, 1977).
Winnett, F.V., 'Re-examining the Foundations', *JBL* 84 (1965), pp. 1-19.
—'The Kerygma of the Yahwist', *Interp* 29 (1966).
Wright, D.R., *Oral Traditions from the Gambia*, Vol. I (Ohio, 1979).
Wundt, W., *Völkerpsychologie*, Vol. II/3 (Leipzig, 1909).
Wyatt, N., 'The Problem of the "Gods of the Fathers"', *ZAW* 90 (1978), pp. 101-104.
Yu, A.C., *Parnassus Revisited* (Chicago, 1973).
Zipes, J., *Fairy Tales and the Art of Subversion* (London, 1983).

INDEX

INDEX OF AUTHORS

Aarne, A. 85, 134n59
Abrahams, R.D. 131n7, 132nn74,79
Albright, W.F. 76, 132n13, 135n103
Alt, A. 34-36, 43, 124n120-27
Andersson, T.M. 75, 132n15, 133n48

Barthes, R. 80, 133n25
Barlett, F.C. 45, 125n189
Barton, J. 131n2
Bascom, W.R. 87-88, 119n14, 134nn71,72
Beidelmann, T.D. 102, 119n2
Ben-Amos, D. 15-17, 89, 91, 119n15, 120nn21,22, 133n34, 134nn75,76,77,79, 135n82
Benson, L.D. 53, 128n13
Birkeland, H. 46-47, 65, 127n199-203

Caird, G.B. 132n16
Childs, B.S. 125n162, 132n12
Coats, G.W. 11, 138n179
Conroy, C. 136n113
Cross, F.M. 74, 93, 131n5
Culley, R.C. 71-72, 101, 127n1, 131nn94,95

Danielson, L. 57, 60, 129n38
Dégh, I. 17, 67, 89, 120n24, 130n73, 134nn80,81
Dollerup, C. 132nn28,29, 133n29
Dorson, R.M. 17, 103-104, 120n23, 121n55, 137n150
Dundes, A. 74, 80, 121n55, 122n65, 131n10, 133n36
Dupré, L. 104, 137n51

Eissfeldt, O. 86, 87, 120n34, 134nn65-70
Ellis, J.M. 78, 112, 126n191, 132n26
Emerton, J.A. 126n185
Engnell, I. 47-48, 50, 65, 127nn204-16
Ewald, H.A. 121n39

Finnegan, R. 53-55, 64-65, 68-69, 71, 88, 107, 123nn84,86, 126n191, 128nn15,17,27,31, 130nn65-67,80,83, 131nn84,87,92,93, 136n108, 138nn165,179
Frazer, J.G. 13-15, 17-18, 27, 79, 119nn1,3,5,6,8,9, 123n85, 133n31
Funk and Wagnall's 15

de Geus, C.H. 126n187
Gilbert, P. 120n25, 132n18
Gomme, G.L. 78-79, 133n30
Goody, J. 64, 130n63
Gray, B. 60, 129nn51,52,58
Gressmann, H. 26, 98, 101, 121n77
Grimm, J.L.C. 23, 38, 73-79, 81, 112, 121nn53-57, 132nn19-22
Gunkel, H. 18, 23-34, 40-41, 49, 57, 64-65, 73, 74, 76-77, 86-90, 97-101, 108, 113, 121n58, 59, 122nn60-64,68-76, 123nn79-83,88-115, 124nn116-26, 131nn3,4, 136nn125-37

Hand, W.D. 14, 54
Hayes, J.H. 122n66, 132n13
Henige, D.P. 110, 137n149, 138n176

Irvin, D. 90-91, 108, 135nn84-101,104,106,107
Irwin, P. 138n168

Jabbour, A. 128n16
Jason, H. 80, 91-96, 136nn109-12, 114-21
Jolles, A. 38, 40, 41, 45, 50, 75, 81-85, 133nn38,40-46

Kelber, W.H. 138n171
Kellogg, R. 59, 129n47
Klatt, W. 120n25, 122n78
Knight, D.H. 45, 121nn49,51, 124n128, 126nn192,193

Knierim, R. 130n67
Koch, K. 66, 68, 124n129, 130n70

Lloyd-Jones, H. 128n28
Lord, A.B. 51-55, 59, 62, 67, 127n3, 128nn4-12,18-26, 129nn48,55,56, 131n91
Lowie, R.H. 45, 126n190

McKane, W. 124n127
McMillan, D.J. 130n82
Miller, J.C. 104, 137nn153-55,159-62
Moore, J.R. 68, 130n82

Nicholson, E.W. 125n162
Nielson, E. 49, 127nn221,222
Noth, M. 34, 41-44, 50, 68, 125nn163-85, 126n186, 130n81
Nyberg, H.S. 46, 65, 126nn194-98

Olrik, A. 25, 45, 50, 55-57, 59-60, 63, 64, 67, 76, 122nn65,67-74, 129nn34,46
Ong, W.J. 64, 130n62
Opland, J. 53, 128n14
Ortutay, G. 89, 121n52, 131n88

Parry, M. 51, 91, 126n2
Pearl, V. 128n28
Pentikäinen, J. 57, 66-68, 80, 129nn39-41, 130nn71,74-78, 133n37, 135n101
Pfeiffer, R.H. 120n34
Propp, U. 75, 79-81, 133n33, 135n101
de Pury, A. 126n185

Rad, G. von 34, 36-41, 44, 50, 101, 124nn138-60
Ranke, K. 75, 85, 134n57
Ritteridge, G.L. 131n85
Rogerson, J.W. 16, 119n19, 131n6

Scheub, H. 137n158
Schmidt, F.W. 129n35
Segal, D. 80
Simpson, C.A. 120n34
Smend, R. 120n34
Stahl, S.K.D. 75
Sydow, C.W. von 66-67, 75, 83, 120n72, 133n50, 134n58

Talmon, S. 134n113
Tannen, D. 64, 128n32, 130n64
Tedlock, D. 56, 70, 129n37
Thoms, W. 15, 119n12
Thompson, S. 16, 75, 85-86, 90, 112, 119n2, 126n188, 127n223, 134nn59,60-64
Thompson, T.C. 137n138
Todorov, T. 74, 97, 131nn8,9, 136n123
Tucker, G.M. 132n17

Utley, F.L. 15-16, 119nn11,17, 133n47

Van Seters, J. 35, 55, 57-59, 61-66, 68, 136n122, 124n127, 129nn33,42-45,57, 130nn59-61,68, 136n124
Vansina, J. 102-103, 107-109, 124n128, 137nn141-48, 138nn164,169,173,174

Warner, S.M. 122n66
Wesselski, J. 132n25
Wellhausen, J. 18-23, 32, 108, 119n10, 120nn28-33,35, 121nn36-38,40-48,50
Westermann, C. 40, 50, 81, 84-55, 109, 133n52, 134nn53-56, 138nn170,173
Widengren, G. 48-49, 127nn217-20
Wilson, R.R. 107, 138n166
Worden, B. 128n28
Wundt, W. 33, 44, 122n78

Zipes, J. 77-78, 112, 132nn23,24

JOURNAL FOR THE STUDY OF THE OLD TESTAMENT
Supplement Series

1. I, HE, WE AND THEY:
   A LITERARY APPROACH TO ISAIAH 53
   D.J.A. Clines
*2. JEWISH EXEGESIS OF THE BOOK OF RUTH
   D.R.G. Beattie
*3. THE LITERARY STRUCTURE OF PSALM 2
   P. Auffret
4. THANKSGIVING FOR A LIBERATED PROPHET:
   AN INTERPRETATION OF ISAIAH CHAPTER 53
   R.N. Whybray
5. REDATING THE EXODUS AND CONQUEST
   J.J. Bimson
6. THE STORY OF KING DAVID:
   GENRE AND INTERPRETATION
   D.M. Gunn
7. THE SENSE OF BIBLICAL NARRATIVE I:
   STRUCTURAL ANALYSES IN THE HEBREW BIBLE (2nd edition)
   D. Jobling
*8. GENESIS 1-11: STUDIES IN STRUCTURE AND THEME
   P.D. Miller
*9. YAHWEH AS PROSECUTOR AND JUDGE:
   AN INVESTIGATION OF THE PROPHETIC LAWSUIT (RIB PATTERN)
   K. Nielsen
10. THE THEME OF THE PENTATEUCH
    D.J.A. Clines
*11. STUDIA BIBLICA 1978 I:
    PAPERS ON OLD TESTAMENT AND RELATED THEMES
    Edited by E.A. Livingstone
12. THE JUST KING:
    MONARCHICAL JUDICIAL AUTHORITY IN ANCIENT ISRAEL
    K.W. Whitelam
13. ISAIAH AND THE DELIVERANCE OF JERUSALEM:
    A STUDY OF THE INTERPRETATION OF PROPHECY
    IN THE OLD TESTAMENT
    R.E. Clements
14. THE FATE OF KING SAUL:
    AN INTERPRETATION OF A BIBLICAL STORY
    D.M. Gunn
15. THE DEUTERONOMISTIC HISTORY
    M. Noth
16. PROPHECY AND ETHICS:
    ISAIAH AND THE ETHICAL TRADITIONS OF ISRAEL
    E.W. Davies
17. THE ROLES OF ISRAEL'S PROPHETS
    D.L. Petersen
18. THE DOUBLE REDACTION OF THE DEUTERONOMISTIC HISTORY
    R.D. Nelson
19. ART AND MEANING: RHETORIC IN BIBLICAL LITERATURE
    Edited by D.J.A. Clines, D.M. Gunn, & A.J. Hauser

20 THE PSALMS OF THE SONS OF KORAH
   M.D. Goulder
21 COLOUR TERMS IN THE OLD TESTAMENT
   A. Brenner
22 AT THE MOUNTAIN OF GOD:
   STORY AND THEOLOGY IN EXODUS 32-34
   R.W.L. Moberly
23 THE GLORY OF ISRAEL:
   THE THEOLOGY AND PROVENIENCE OF THE ISAIAH TARGUM
   B.D. Chilton
24 MIDIAN, MOAB AND EDOM:
   THE HISTORY AND ARCHAEOLOGY OF LATE BRONZE AND IRON AGE
   JORDAN AND NORTH-WEST ARABIA
   Edited by J.F.A. Sawyer & D.J.A Clines
25 THE DAMASCUS COVENANT:
   AN INTERPRETATION OF THE 'DAMASCUS DOCUMENT'
   P.R. Davies
26 CLASSICAL HEBREW POETRY:
   A GUIDE TO ITS TECHNIQUES
   W.G.E. Watson
27 PSALMODY AND PROPHECY
   W.H. Bellinger
28 HOSEA: AN ISRAELITE PROPHET IN JUDEAN PERSPECTIVE
   G.I. Emmerson
29 EXEGESIS AT QUMRAN:
   4QFLORILEGIUM IN ITS JEWISH CONTEXT
   G.J. Brooke
30 THE ESTHER SCROLL: THE STORY OF THE STORY
   D.J.A. Clines
31 IN THE SHELTER OF ELYON:
   ESSAYS IN HONOR OF G.W. AHLSTRÖM
   Edited by W.B. Barrick & J.R. Spencer
32 THE PROPHETIC PERSONA:
   JEREMIAH AND THE LANGUAGE OF THE SELF
   T. Polk
33 LAW AND THEOLOGY IN DEUTERONOMY
   J.G. McConville
34 THE TEMPLE SCROLL:
   AN INTRODUCTION, TRANSLATION AND COMMENTARY
   J. Maier
35 SAGA, LEGEND, TALE, NOVELLA, FABLE:
   NARRATIVE FORMS IN OLD TESTAMENT LITERATURE
   Edited by G.W. Coats
36 THE SONG OF FOURTEEN SONGS
   M.D. Goulder
37 UNDERSTANDING THE WORD:
   ESSAYS IN HONOR OF BERNHARD W. ANDERSON
   Edited by J.T. Butler, E.W. Conrad & B.C. Ollenburger
38 SLEEP, DIVINE AND HUMAN, IN THE OLD TESTAMENT
   T.H. McAlpine
39 THE SENSE OF BIBLICAL NARRATIVE II:
   STRUCTURAL ANALYSES IN THE HEBREW BIBLE
   D. Jobling

40 DIRECTIONS IN BIBLICAL HEBREW POETRY
    Edited by E.R. Follis
41 ZION, THE CITY OF THE GREAT KING:
    A THEOLOGICAL SYMBOL OF THE JERUSALEM CULT
    B.C. Ollenburger
42 A WORD IN SEASON: ESSAYS IN HONOUR OF WILLIAM McKANE
    Edited by J.D. Martin & P.R. Davies
43 THE CULT OF MOLEK:
    A REASSESSMENT
    G.C. Heider
44 THE IDENTITY OF THE INDIVIDUAL IN THE PSALMS
    S.J.L. Croft
45 THE CONFESSIONS OF JEREMIAH IN CONTEXT:
    SCENES OF PROPHETIC DRAMA
    A.R. Diamond
46 THE BOOK OF THE JUDGES: AN INTEGRATED READING
    B.G. Webb
47 THE GREEK TEXT OF JEREMIAH:
    A REVISED HYPOTHESIS
    S. Soderlund
48 TEXT AND CONTEXT:
    OLD TESTAMENT AND SEMITIC STUDIES FOR F.C. FENSHAM
    Edited by W. Claassen
49 THEOPHORIC PERSONAL NAMES IN ANCIENT HEBREW
    J.D. Fowler
50 THE CHRONICLER'S HISTORY
    M. Noth
51 DIVINE INITIATIVE AND HUMAN RESPONSE IN EZEKIEL
    P. Joyce
52 THE CONFLICT OF FAITH AND EXPERIENCE IN THE PSALMS:
    A FORM-CRITICAL AND THEOLOGICAL STUDY
    C.C. Broyles
53 THE MAKING OF THE PENTATEUCH:
    A METHODOLOGICAL STUDY
    R.N. Whybray
54 FROM REPENTANCE TO REDEMPTION:
    JEREMIAH'S THOUGHT IN TRANSITION
    J. Unterman
55 THE ORIGIN TRADITION OF ANCIENT ISRAEL:
    THE LITERARY FORMATION OF GENESIS AND EXODUS 1-23
    T.L. Thompson
56 THE PURIFICATION OFFERING IN THE PRIESTLY LITERATURE:
    ITS MEANING AND FUNCTION
    N. Kiuchi
57 MOSES: HEROIC MAN, MAN OF GOD
    G.W. Coats
58 THE LISTENING HEART: ESSAYS IN WISDOM AND THE PSALMS
    IN HONOR OF ROLAND E. MURPHY, O. CARM.
    Edited by K.G. Hoglund
59 CREATIVE BIBLICAL EXEGESIS:
    CHRISTIAN AND JEWISH HERMENEUTICS THROUGH THE CENTURIES
    B. Uffenheimer & H.G. Reventlow

60 HER PRICE IS BEYOND RUBIES:
   THE JEWISH WOMAN IN GRAECO-ROMAN PALESTINE
   L.J. Archer
61 FROM CHAOS TO RESTORATION:
   AN INTEGRATIVE READING OF ISAIAH 24–27
   D.G. Johnson
62 THE OLD TESTAMENT AND FOLKLORE STUDY
   P.G. Kirkpatrick
63 SHILOH: A BIBLICAL CITY IN TRADITION AND HISTORY
   D.G. Schley
64 TO SEE AND NOT PERCEIVE:
   ISAIAH 6.9-10 IN EARLY JEWISH AND CHRISTIAN INTERPRETATION
   C.A. Evans
65 THERE IS HOPE FOR A TREE:
   THE TREE AS METAPHOR IN ISAIAH
   K. Nielsen
66 THE SECRETS OF THE TIMES:
   RECOVERING BIBLICAL CHRONOLOGIES
   J. Hughes

* Out of print